It's A Wild Life

II

It's A Wild Life

By

William Wasserman

ISBN 978-0-9718907-3-2

Cover by Timothy Flanigan

ALSO BY WILLIAM WASSERMAN

Track of the Poacher

Wildlife Guardian

Game Warden

Poacher Wars

Pennsylvania Wildlife Tails

Trapping Secrets

Beaver Trapping and Snaring Methods

Muskrat and Mink Trapping

For Jenna and Matthew

Introduction

As a Pennsylvania Game Warden for more than three decades, I patrolled four hundred square miles of rugged mountain terrain where I pursued poachers on foot and by vehicle and boat. Along the way, I investigated thousands of game law violations and arrested many violent career poachers.

But another huge part of my job was in the public relations and education field where I represented my agency by speaking before sportsmen's clubs, schools, conventions, fairs, church groups and many other organizations. I also wrote a weekly newspaper column titled *It's a Wild Life*. Hence, the title of this book, which contains twenty-six columns chosen from more than seven hundred that were published over a fifteen year period. They run the gamut from confrontations with poachers and game hogs to stories about animal survival, free roaming pets, captive wildlife, and unpredictable encounters with wild critters.

The stories are based on my memories over a period of years and may differ from the memories of others. I also admit to taking some creative liberties with events and to re-creating some of the dialog. I have also given the poachers and their associates fictitious names and have altered their physical descriptions. Any resemblance to actual persons, living or dead is entirely coincidental.

Listen! The wind is rising,
And the air is wild with leaves…
— Humbert Wolfe

*The bold ones continue. They are eyed by the eagles; the
lightning plays about them: the hurricane is furious. No
matter, they persevere.*
    ~Victor Hugo

The Outlaw and the Boy

THE OUTLAW CRADLED HIS RIFLE in his arms and
strolled down the railroad tracks with a pocket full of hollow
point bullets. There was a bounce in his step as he walked, for
he loved to shoot things, and the railroad afforded him many
targets both living and dead.

The iron rails stretched for forty miles along the east bank
of the Susquehanna River as they made their way from the
deep south all the way to Maine. Trains almost never used this
branch, and local nature lovers often walked the railroad
enjoying the spectacular countryside. Occasional thrill seekers
ran their ATVs and dirt bikes along the graveled berm on each
side of the tracks as well, racing along at full throttle for miles
on end. But most folks preferred to simply walk the rails, some
stopping to fish the neighboring river for walleyes and bass,
while others enjoyed scavenging for old bottles and other
treasures that washed up along its silted banks.

There is something about a railroad that seems to draw
people. To some, the steel rails represent a sense of freedom
as they meander seemingly forever through town and country
and into grand and bustling cities. Every bend in the tracks
whispers of secret places ahead, beckoning you onward. And
too, there is always the possibility of a train looming from

around a bend. It could be on you in seconds. A thousand tons of hulking steel. Unstoppable. Perhaps that's part of the lure—that lurking danger that might be somewhere just ahead, out of sight, then suddenly hurtling toward you at breakneck speed.

For The Outlaw the railroad was simply an isolated area where he could shoot at river rats as they scavenged the surrounding cornfields for leftovers from autumn's harvest. But it was late afternoon and the rats had come and gone, so in their place he would pick off a few songbirds and the occasional squirrel or rabbit that might present itself. They would be shot on sight. Their bodies left where they fell. Ah, yes, there was nothing like a living, breathing, honest-to-goodness warm target—and every living creature would be a potential victim for his gun. For every life he took empowered him all the more.

The boy raced across his back yard and stopped at the edge of his property to gaze at the river far below. It looked like a thin ribbon as it wound its way through the distant mountains, its frigid water glistening like diamonds under a brilliant March sky. It was the first mild day in five long months. And although patches of snow still lingered in isolated shady spots, the wind was absent today, the sun so warm on his freckled cheeks it felt like summer might be just around the corner.

It was Saturday. No school and no homework to worry about. What's more, the bass had been biting all week according to local gossip. And with that delightful thought in mind, the boy raced down the hill toward the river, a fishing rod in one hand and a soup can full of squirming night crawlers in the other.

When he reached the bottom, he crossed a macadam state road and hurried through the woods until he came to a clearing where the railroad tracks broke through. Stepping into the center of the rails, he gazed across a broad cornfield, its stalks reduced to brown stubble by an enormous grain harvester months ago. Beyond the cornfield lay the river. And if he followed the tracks north, they would take him to the cove, a secret place where the fish were eager to accommodate his hook.

He dropped to his hands and knees and put an ear to the iron rail. The rail was silent, no sign of any trains, so the boy stood and began walking north along the tracks, making certain to step on every wooden tie for good luck as he went.

There was a sharp bend a quarter-mile ahead, impossible to see around. Here the tracks were bordered on the right by a hill of jagged rock, to the left a fierce vertical wall of granite descended two hundred feet to the river below, forming a cove where a gentle eddy pooled. Even on the coldest winter days, the boy would be shielded from the icy winds. And it was here that the fish would come to rest, for the easy water protected them from the river's powerful current.

As the boy continued toward the bend, he came across dozens of .22 caliber casings lying in the gravel between the ties. Some with their brass coatings darkened to a dull brown over time, others so new they sparkled like tiny gold nuggets in the sun.

Wyoming County was rural. Most folks had guns, and many were avid hunters just like his dad. The fact that someone had been shooting here didn't surprise him at all, but he wondered what they were targeting. There were no tin cans or bottles lying about, and there were too many empty casings to be from a hunter's gun. He was about to move on when he looked up at the telegraph poles lining the tracks to his right and saw the glass insulators had been shot off their crossbeams. He frowned with disapproval, for it seemed senseless to vandalize property like that. The poles had lined the tracks for more than fifty years, and it was like destroying a part of history.

But the damage had been done, and there was nothing he could do to change it, so he continued down the tracks once again, being mindful to step on every wooden tie for good luck.

He didn't get far when he saw a dead blue jay lying on the gravel berm by the woods on his left. Curious, he laid his fishing rod and worms on the tracks and walked over for a closer look. It lay on its back, the white feathers of its breast speckled with crimson flecks of blood. He stooped and picked up the bird, its tiny head rolling sideways in his palm, the body still warm. He parted its breast feathers with a thumb and saw a small hole in its fragile chest.

The boy suspected that whomever had been shooting the glass insulators had also killed the jay. And the nasty feeling that he might be somewhere close by, watching him, sent an icy chill down his spine. He whipped his head left and right, hoping someone wasn't hiding behind a tree with a gun pointed at his back. Then he spun on his heels and looked behind him. But there was no one. And he chuckled to himself for letting his mind play devilish tricks on him like that.

The boy walked a short distance into the woods with the blue jay in his hand and looked for a place to bury it. He saw a softball-sized rock partially frozen into the ground and got down on his knees and pried it loose with his hands. He laid the bird in the depression and marveled at its beauty. He'd seen plenty of blue jays before, but never this close. On its head was a perky crest of feathers, and the blue coloring on its wings and tail were tinged with vibrant bars of black and white. Such a terrible waste of life. He scraped a handful of matted leaves from the forest floor and covered the bird with them, then he gently placed the rock over the leaves to seal its grave.

He wished he could have given it a decent burial, but the ground was still too hard. This would just have to do. So he whispered a short prayer over the bird and then stood and walked back to the railroad tracks. He started toward the bend once again, and although his mood had turned somber, he was still mindful to step on every wooden tie for good luck along the way.

Then, as he neared the bend, he heard a high-pitched whistling from above. The boy looked into the brilliant sapphire sky and stared in awe as a majestic bald eagle soared above on broad, flattened wings, the snow-white feathers of its head and tail ablaze in the golden sun.

16

He watched as the eagle set its wings and glided toward a tall oak at the edge of the bend. As it reached the tree, it extended its legs and grasped a stout limb with talons powerful enough to crush a man's hand. The eagle perched there, statue-like, and inspected the eddy below with eyes that could see five times farther than a human can. The boy was amazed by its presence. This was the first eagle he'd ever seen, and he smiled with the realization that it knew one of the best fishing spots in the river, just as he did.

The Outlaw roamed the tracks like a hungry predator searching for prey, rifle at the ready, a long and boney finger caressing its trigger as he searched the terrain for new targets. There were no telegraph poles here, no glass insulators to shoot from their posts. Nor were there any discarded cans or bottles lying about like he saw along the local roadways. In fact, he hadn't fired his rifle since killing that stupid bird a while back, and he was getting bored.

The bird had been an irritation. Flitting from tree to tree with its jeering cries and endless string of clicks, clucks and whistles. Good grief! What noise! And worse yet, it seemed to be scolding him. Staring at him with its beady black eyes as if it had more rights than he did. What a joke! He chuckled inside as he thought back on it. Shooting it and putting it out of its misery had been a blessing.

But putting a bullet through the bird's chest had only intensified his desire to kill. Tin cans and bottles would do in a pinch, but what he really wanted was another live target, something that might present more of a challenge this time.

And it was at that precise moment that he heard the piercing cry of the eagle. His mood brightened as he watched it fold its massive wings and settle upon the oak. What a magnificent trophy it would make! Its wingspan had to be six feet across. And wasn't luck with him today, for it was well within range of his rifle and never noticed him, for its attention was focused on the river far below.

The Outlaw didn't concern himself with the fact that eagles were an endangered species or that they embody the national emblem of our country. Nor did he concern himself with the notion that to most Americans the fierce beauty of a bald eagle represents the strength of our nation and the indomitable spirit of its people, as well as the freedom, peace and prosperity that we are all so privileged to enjoy. But had he reflected on these truths, he would have shot it just the same. And perhaps, with this profound understanding, enjoyed its slaying all the more.

His eyes brightened as he slowly shouldered his rifle and took aim. The eagle was seventy yards away, an easy shot for such a skilled marksman as he. And when his crosshairs found their mark, he curled a grim finger around the trigger, exhaled slowly through his nose, and squeezed.

The hollow point bullet traveled at supersonic speed, its fatal echo ricocheting off the surrounding mountains long after it had exited the eagle's skull. Death was instantaneous, and as the great raptor fell, The Outlaw raised his rifle triumphantly and let out a resounding whoop of joy.

The boy watched in utter horror as the eagle tumbled from its perch, its lifeless body glancing off limbs as it plummeted gracelessly to the ground and landed on the graveled berm by the tracks.

He stood frozen in shock, his brain barely able to absorb what had happened. It seemed impossible. Like a bad dream. Only it was real. All too real.

And when a ragged cry of jubilation came from around the bend, fear struck his heart like a steel fist. It was him! Just ahead! The one who had killed the jay! And now the eagle! His throat thickened, his breathing all but impossible. Something bad was coming his way. This he knew instinctively. And he was terrified.

Run! his mind screamed. *Run! He's going to get you!*

And he would have, but for that adventurous, bulletproof, I'm-young-and-invincible mindset that's inherent in every boy ever born. And it held him there like a deer frozen in the headlights of an oncoming semi.

Then he saw The Outlaw. He stormed from around the bend, rifle in hand, his gaze focused on his obscene kill. So focused, in fact, that at first he never noticed the boy. But as he bent over to reach for his prize, he froze suddenly and quickly looked up.

The distance of a football field separated them. A contrast of Good and Evil. The Outlaw's eyes narrowed into angry slits as he slowly came erect, his face twisted into an angry scowl of contempt.

"YOU!" he cried. *"GET OVER HERE RIGHT NOW!"*

He held his rifle casually at his hip with the barrel pointed toward the boy. Fearing for his life, the boy glanced frantically from side to side. The hill to his right was steep and impossible. To his left lay the river. Although the drop to the water would be fatal from where The Outlaw stood, the terrain alongside the boy was level and wooded before descending to the river in a gradual slope. If he ran fast enough he could make it to the river in a matter of seconds, then he would slide down the long bank to the river's edge and work his way to the cove where he could hide and be safe.

"YOU BOY!" roared The Outlaw. "DON'T MAKE ME COME AFTER YOU!"

The Outlaw took a step forward, and the boy suddenly found his legs. Dropping his fishing rod and worms on the tracks, he ran for the river as fast as he could.

The world fell silent around him as he fled, his mind focused solely on escape. He could hear the blood coursing through his veins, the rapid beat of his heart, his steady breathing. Nothing else. He zigzagged left and right through the woods like an NFL tailback through an opposing team, feet pummeling the ground as he dodged trees and rocks, leaping over fallen logs and dead branches like Superman (*faster than a speeding bullet, more powerful than a locomotive, able to leap tall buildings in a single bound*), except unlike the famed superhero from the comics he adored, the boy was scared to death.

In less than a minute he reached the cliff's edge, threw his legs straight out from under him, and began sliding down the two-hundred-foot slope on his back—but realized at once that he was plunging to his death.

Recent snowmelt had caused the river to rise, the icy waters turning dark and treacherous. Sliding flat out, he flipped over on his belly and clawed wildly at the frozen ground, reaching for anything that might break his fall, but there were only tufts of straw-like grass that snapped off in thick clumps as he grabbed for them.

He closed his eyes and gritted his teeth, expecting to plunge into the river at any moment when a rock protruding from the bank caught his knee, sending a stabbing pain deep to the bone before ripping across his chest. He quickly reached for it, almost dislocating his shoulders as fingers like steel talons gripped its jagged edge to break his fall.

He held on for dear life, heart hammering in his chest as the turbulent river swirled inches from his feet. And his heart sank when he realized that his escape route to the cove was under six feet of water.

"God...please..."

A sudden sprinkle of pebbles rolled down the bank, inches from his face, before plopping into the river. The boy craned his neck to look up, and his stomach tightened into a sickening knot. For although the sun was in his eyes, almost blinding him, he could see the dark profile of The Outlaw. He was standing at the edge of the precipice, rifle in his hand as he looked down at him.

The boy whipped his head toward the cove a hundred yards away. It was his only hope. Although the decline had been sharp and barren where he had slid down, it was much less severe and walkable just twenty yards ahead. Thick saplings grew there, too. They'd make good cover as he worked his way to the cove. But twenty yards might as well be twenty miles if he couldn't get there.

Dozens of rocks poked from the ground in every direction across the slippery bank. They were smaller than the one that had saved him from the fall, but big enough to gain hold of. So he began to inch his way toward the cove like an elite Sherpa mountaineer, clutching at the rocks with his hands while purchasing a toehold where he could on the rocky surface.

As he pulled himself along, he saw a flat rock protruding from the bank big enough to accommodate his entire foot. It would be a stretch, but if he reached it, he could rest for a moment. The boy inched his left leg along the bank until he made contact with the rock, but when he put his full weight down, an electric shock ran from his knee all the way to his hip socket, and he cried out in pain. He could feel a wet coating on his calf, too. It was blood, and he worried that he might not make it to the cove after all.

Steeling himself against the throbbing pain in his leg, his face pressed against the damp hillside, he reached out with his left arm and grabbed the point of a rock jutting from the ground. Digging his fingers into its grainy edge, he held tight while extending his injured leg along the surface of the hillside to a larger rock below him and carefully let the full weight of his body settle once again. A numbing pain wormed its way up his thigh, but he gritted his teeth and pushed on until he finally made it to the tree line that would lead him to safety.

Reaching out to grab a sapling, he held it for support and stepped onto a ledge that served as a deer trail. The boy had used it many times before on his way to the cove. Aware that the trail snaked its way down from the railroad above, he glanced nervously over his shoulder to the hilltop. His pursuer was gone. But he would find the trail, too. He could be coming for him right now. The boy envisioned him pointing his terrible gun. He imagined a bullet striking him from behind, his body sprawled lifeless on the cold ground.

He had to run. Bad leg or not, he had to run.

The boy hobbled along the crooked deer path as best he could, his injured knee shouting at him with every step. It was impossible to put his full weight on his leg, and he was moving much too slow. He glanced over his shoulder as he shuffled toward the cove, breathing a sigh of relief when he saw no one following him.

Rounding a bend in the path, he saw a narrow animal trail that came from the river and led into the surrounding woods. Beavers had been feeding on poplar saplings here, their trail littered with remnant twigs. To his right, several downed trees had been felled by the giant rodents. Most of the branches had been gnawed off and dragged back to the river, but a few still lay scattered about. He spotted one stout limb about four feet long, the bark peeled clean and the wood hardened to a boney white pole. He limped over and picked it up. Then, using it as a makeshift crutch, the boy continued toward the cove at a much faster pace.

The Outlaw strode down the deer trail at a steady measured gait as he scanned the woods for a glimpse of the kid. He was an expert tracker and a skilled marksman. And although he'd hunted hundreds of birds and animals in his time, this was his first human. The kid proved to be quite a challenge, too. The slide down the hillside was ingenious, and completely unexpected. And had he not cracked his knee on that rock, he might have gotten away. But now it was just a matter of time.

He was impressed with the kid's agility, too. Watching him scale the rocky hillside while hanging on for dear life was a treat. He expected to see him fall. And had the rocks not been frozen into the ground, the kid would have taken a tumble for sure. He was a lucky boy. A few more days with weather like this and the rocks would have pulled free with his weight, sending him plunging into the river. And with the combination of his bum knee along with the raging current and frigid water, he'd have been gone in a matter of seconds. Which would have been too bad.

The kid really took the bait when he deepened his voice into a fearsome howl back at tracks. Scared him out of his wits.

Don't make me come after you!

Worked like a charm. Only he'd expected him to run uphill toward the state road, hoping to flag down a passing motorist. But he would have stopped him long before he made it to the top. The kid was fast but not that fast. Still this longer version…this extended hunt, so to speak, would be so much more enjoyable. How did that old chewing gum commercial go? Double your pleasure, double your fun?

Yes! That was it.

There was a cove not too far away. That's where the kid would be headed. But the cove was surrounded by a cliff wall, and the kid would be stuck there, shivering in his boots, waiting for the inevitable.

And The Outlaw *was* the inevitable, and it was just a matter of time before he reached him. A very short time indeed.

The boy had been hunting salamanders for bait last summer when he stumbled upon a cave near the mouth of the cove. It wasn't a real cave like the ones he saw on TV or read about in books. It was more like a crevice, actually. Created millions of years ago when the earth had shifted to form a narrow opening between the ground and a boulder the size of a Cadillac. It would be a tight squeeze, but if he turned his head sideways, the space would be just big enough to squirm into.

He knew The Outlaw was coming. He could feel his presence as he lay sprawled in the leaves peering into the dark depression beneath the boulder. It smelled musty in there, like dirty socks, and he worried there might be snakes. The cove was infested with rattlers and copperheads. But it had been a cold winter, and if any snakes lived under the boulder they'd probably be down inside one of the cracks that penetrated its earthen floor. There were several, and he thought they probably led to some mysterious subterranean world where all cold-blooded reptiles dwelled. They might even go all the way to the center of the earth for all he knew.

Still, just to be safe, he took his makeshift crutch in both hands, shoved one end into the opening, and started scraping it over the ground to scare off any snakes that might be lurking inside. He was only at it for a few seconds when he stopped suddenly.

A cold breeze had come his way. There and gone in seconds. His body chilled to the core. Then a great stillness came over the forest, a void if you will, as if the earth had suddenly stopped spinning.

He was here.

The boy threw his pole inside the chamber and searched for something to cover the opening once he was inside. He saw a tree limb lying on the ground nearby. It was big—bigger than a man's leg. Limping over, he dragged it back to the opening. Then he dropped to his belly and reached into the mouth of the crevice, groping frantically for something to latch hold of. He felt a stout root and wrapped his fingers tightly around it. Using it for leverage, he turned his head sideways and pulled with all his might, squirming into the chamber like a tadpole into mud. Turning quickly, he reached back outside and pulled the limb against the opening, the outside world becoming visible through a thin gap between the top of the limb and the roof of his hideout. Then he pressed his face against its knotty bark and peered out the narrow opening.

Suddenly he saw him.

He moved down the path in an easy, rolling gate, his head in the air like a wolf searching for the scent of its prey. He was clean-shaven with piercing eyes, high cheekbones, and a ponytail that fell to his shoulders. He wore a heavy plaid shirt with denim jeans and black leather boots, and carried his rifle casually in his right hand at the balance point, as if he knew the chase was coming to an end.

The boy watched him walk to the edge of the cove. He stood there for what seemed an eternity, gazing at the swirling water below. Then he shielded his eyes with a flattened hand and looked up the vertical stone wall to the tree where the eagle had been. Nodding his head as if struck by some newfound knowledge, he pivoted slowly and stood facing the boulder.

The boy shrank back into his chamber and curled into a fetal position, his heart pounding so loudly he thought the man might hear it. His chest felt like it was in a vice, his breathing came only in ragged puffs. He wanted to wiggle down one of the cracks in the ground. Snakes or not, he would have if only he could. But there was no escape. He had trapped himself under this giant rock, and now it would serve as a headstone where his bones would lie until someone discovered them one day. If ever.

He tried not to cry but the tears came streaming down his cheeks just the same, his throat so tight he couldn't utter a sound, his sobs coming only as a mute and convulsive shuddering of his chest.

He could hear his approaching footsteps, the crunch of his terrible boots as he neared. He stared wide-eyed at the narrow spear of light that entered his dark cocoon between the limb and the boulder. His window to the outside world. And he trembled when it was cut off by his pursuer's grim shadow. He squeezed his eyes tight, his face a grimace of impending doom.

And he prayed.

Time came to a standstill. For how long he could not say. Minutes? Hours? An eternity? But at its final passage, he felt a peaceful calm wash over him, and he slowly opened his eyes. A thin shaft of light peeked into the darkness once again. And in the distance, he could hear his fading footsteps as they drifted farther and farther away. He waited until long after they were gone, then he pushed the limb from the mouth of his cave and crawled out the narrow opening. He stood slowly, blinking into the dazzling sunlight. A gentle southerly breeze kissed his cheek, and birds chirped and gurgled merrily among the surrounding canopy of trees.

And as sure as he could sense his presence before, he felt his absence now. He was safe. Finally, he was safe.

When I got the call about an eagle that had just been shot along the Susquehanna River, it hit me like a fist in the guts. In those days eagles were about as common as rainbows on the moon, and I went immediately to the informant's house to interview him. A father and his freckle-faced son greeted me as I stepped up to the front door. And although the phone call had come from the father, I soon learned that the person I'd be interviewing would be a twelve-year-old boy. I was invited into their home and sat with them in the living room where I listened in awe to the boy's incredible story.

When he finished, I thanked them both for contacting me and drove down to the railroad tracks hoping I might apprehend the person responsible for the shooting. I realized that my odds were slim at best, but I had a clear description of the man, and I radioed a BOLO (Be on the Lookout) to several of my deputies directing them to patrol a five mile perimeter of the railroad.

I parked my patrol car along the tracks near where the boy said he'd found brass casings from a .22 caliber firearm and walked up to rails. I found everything exactly as he had described. Someone had been doing a lot of shooting. Most of the insulators were shot off the telegraph poles here, and dozens of spent casings littered the tracks.

From there, I walked directly toward the distant bend in the tracks, stopping along the way when I found a soup can lying on its side between the rails. Most of the contents had spilled to the gravel. The worms, unable to penetrate the hardpan, withered from the sun. I looked around for a fishing rod but never found one. Then I stepped off the rails and walked through the woods to the river's edge. I gazed down the long and sloping bank and saw a narrow trail of curved grass stretching to the raging river below, just as the boy had indicated.

I walked back to the tracks and proceeded toward the bend. As I came close, I could see something lying by the rails in the otherwise distinctively flat berm. I continued walking, knowing what I'd find long before I reached it.

The eagle that once had played here lay dead.

Years passed before he returned to the tracks. Flashbacks of the man and his gun still lingered in his mind as if it were yesterday. It terrified him to think of it. But he knew that to conquer his fear, to find peace, he must go back. And he chose to do that on an unusually warm day in March. A day when the sky was sapphire blue under a brilliant midday sun and a warm breeze from the south was at his back.

Not much had changed now that he was in his twenties. The same cornfields bordered the tracks to his left as he walked toward the bend, their stalks reduced to rows of brown stubble by the giant grain harvester. To his right, the familiar old telegraph poles lined the tracks like ancient Roman crosses. And in the distance, he could see the bend. His journey's end. The place he needed to be.

He chuckled to himself when he realized he'd been unconsciously stepping on every wooden tie as he walked, and thought perhaps there was something to that silly old custom after all.

As he neared the bend, he saw that the towering oak where the eagle had been was now dead. Most of its branches broken off years ago, the once magnificent tree reduced to a hollow snag as if poisoned by some foul misdeed. And it was then that a jolt of pain suddenly gripped his knee, the same knee he'd injured on that day so long ago. He stopped and massaged it with both hands. And as the throbbing began to subside, he realized he was standing where he had jumped the tracks to run to the river on that fateful day. He stepped off the tracks, easing his weight on his leg to see if the pain would return. And when it did not, he walked through the woods to the river's steep edge.

There was no flood today. The river sparkled and flashed under a blazing midday sun as it rolled south to the Chesapeake Bay. He stared down at the rocks that had saved him from the treacherous waters that day. He remembered how he'd inched his way across the steep and slippery hillside, how he'd fled through the woods and squirmed under the boulder and lay trembling with dread inside its dark chamber. And how he feared it would be his grave.

He pressed a hand against the front pocket of his jeans and felt the heavy steel frame of a derringer pistol. Then he turned and started toward the railroad once again.

DON'T MAKE ME COME AFTER YOU!

The voice came to him as he walked the tracks, as he knew it would. An echo in his mind that shook him to his core. And although fear clutched at his heart, he pushed on, careful to step on every wooden tie as he went.

When he reached the bend, he stood in watchful silence looking north and south along the tracks. He could see for miles each way. But there was no sign of him. So he waited. How long, he did not know, for it was as if time had come to a standstill. And when a cold and fated breeze came suddenly from behind to chill him to the bone, he turned to face it.

But there was only the wind, and the wind passed, and with it his fear.

And he was free. Finally, he was free.

(This story is based on the shooting of a bald eagle along the Susquehanna River in 1995. The case remains unsolved.)

Tell me what are the prevailing sentiments that occupy the minds of your young men, and I will tell you what is to be the character of the next generation.
   ~Edmund Burke

On Virtue

I HAVE ALWAYS CONSIDERED the first day of September to be the unofficial end of summer in northeastern Pennsylvania. Schools are open, nights turn chilly, and the sun isn't as intense any more—even on warm days. It also marks the beginning of hunting season with the opening for mourning doves followed by Canada goose season in mid-month. Pressure for neither species is much to talk about; however, a few hunters can always be found if you know where to look.

As the days melt into weeks followed by months, hunting pressure continues to build. The opener for squirrel and grouse follows archery deer season in early October. Soon after, the general small game season arrives with pheasant and rabbit hunters taking to the fields. Wild turkey and waterfowl seasons are both in full swing by then, and bear hunters will be counting the days until their long-awaited five-day rifle opener begins. Trapping season for land animals merges with everything else, and the opening day for mink, muskrat and beaver is just around the corner. Momentum builds until the statewide deer season opens in late November, and that's when things really get rolling. Along with the increase in hunting pressure each week, poaching activity begins to escalate, and game wardens are run ragged trying to keep up with all the calls and complaints concerning everything from roadkilled deer to illegal night hunting.

With the changing seasons comes a change in attitudes for some folks as well. They become ill-tempered and at times downright hostile. I see it every year. Perhaps it's because more hunters afield means more competition for the available game, which equates to a higher percentage of general grumpiness. Unfortunately, deer season brings out the worst in some people, their desire to bag a buck at any cost transforming them from decent law-abiding citizens into outright villains much like the infamous Jekyll and Hyde.

Don't get me wrong. We still have plenty of honest-to-goodness sportsmen out there. Many are willing to report a poacher even if it means losing valuable hunting time in the process. But there are far too many folks who know of hunters who shoot deer illegally and refuse to get involved. Then, when they pound the woods for days and can't find a nice buck to shoot, they fault their natural resource agency for mismanaging the deer herd. But that's almost never the case. Most times it's the very people they're protecting by not reporting them to the game warden who are to blame.

Many hunters tend to rationalize taking over the limit of game by convincing themselves that one extra deer doesn't make much difference in the grand scheme of things. Their thinking goes something like this: *I didn't get my buck last year, so, technically, I should be allowed to kill two this year...besides, it's the guys who go out at night with spotlights and shoot deer that are the real poachers, not me!*

But in many instances, illegal night shooters are no more a threat to the deer population then the hunter who shoots a deer and puts his buddy's tag on it. It's still an illegal kill, and it can have a huge impact on the overall deer population. With over ten million hunters in the U.S., if only one percent kills an illegal deer each year, it would add up to a hundred-thousand annually, ballooning to one million illegal kills within a decade.

So, as you can see, what we do as individuals actually does matter. That extra pheasant, rabbit or deer really does make a difference; therefore, it behooves the true sportsmen to hone his integrity to its finest level. One way to accomplish this is by imagining you're hunting in front of an audience. If the world were watching, would you pull the trigger? If the world were watching, would you do the right thing and report that poacher?

Any game warden will tell you that most poaching cases are brought to light through information received from the public. The bulk of my investigations over the years began with a phone call from a concerned sportsman; otherwise, the incident would never have been exposed. In most instances, my informants remained anonymous, as I was able to put together a solid case by collecting evidence at the crime scene followed by an interrogation of the suspected poacher. There were only a handful of incidents in my long career where I needed an informant to testify in court—and I prosecuted over a thousand cases.

Every year I see thousands of hunters as they drive to their favorite hunting grounds. I see them with their special Wildlife Resource license plates, their NRA decals, and their bumper stickers proclaiming memberships in various hunting fraternities. And I often wonder how many folks deem those synthetic symbols a sufficient contribution toward the enhancement of our hunting heritage.

I wonder too, how many will have the courage to stop what they're doing and report a game law violation the next time they see one. After all, that one simple act could mean more for our wildlife resource than all the bumper stickers money can buy.

Published March 1991

Laws are felt only when the individual comes into conflict with them.
    ~Suzanne LaFollette

Killer of Innocents

HE MADE HIS WAY SLOWLY up the steep mountain pass. Not because he was too tired or too old to move faster, for he could outmaneuver most men half his age, but because hunting wasn't about the kill anymore as it had been in his younger days so long ago. He moved slowly so he could sense the miracle of God's creation come alive all around him: the earthy smell of the forest's rich soil infused with the scent of white pine, a ruffed grouse drumming its wings deep in the awakening forest, turkeys gobbling in a distant hollow, the festive chatter of gray squirrels and the cheerful melody of mockingbirds and warblers in the branches above.

Although spring gobbler season had been open for two weeks, he'd been too busy with his job to break away. But today would be different. He would hunt for a few hours. A passion he had enjoyed since boyhood when his father would take him along.

And it was the remembrance of those days combined with his enduring love for the outdoors that had determined his future as a steward of our natural resources. Although dressed like any other hunter in the woods, he was a state game warden, just as he had been, every minute of every day, for more than twenty-five years.

He walked for a half-mile in the dim shadows of the forest before reaching his destination: a tall white oak centered on a leaf-covered plateau in the open woods. He sat with his back nestled against its heavy bark and watched in awe as a crimson line began to peek above the horizon and melt the gray dawn. Eyes that have seen the sun rise in the east ten-thousand times before, beamed with joy as the forest slowly brightened, for to him it was one of the most satisfying moments of a day's hunt.

The warden used his box call to create a series of low clucks and soft purrs imitating a hen turkey, its forlorn cry echoing through the woods, begging company. But his eyes and ears were focused on more than the prospect of harvesting a bird. On constant alert for outlaws, his outings invariably became a combination of both hunting and surveillance. And so he listened as the morning stirred all around him. And he watched.

The poacher worked his way up the mountain pass just as the sun began to rise. It was a late start, but he never liked the idea of wandering through the woods in the dark, anyway. A fella could get hurt that way, maybe even lost. Now that the sun was up, it would help take the chill out of the air, too. Considering it was early May, he couldn't believe how cold the morning had been. When was it ever going to warm up? The white frost on his lawn almost made him turn back inside for a second cup of coffee, but time was short, so he jumped into his pickup truck and drove to the mountain instead.

He had one single purpose in mind today: kill a turkey and get back home before the game started this afternoon. His buddies were stopping by later with a keg of beer, expecting to watch the game on his new fifty-inch flat screen. Life didn't get much better than that—except, of course, if he could claim bragging rights to a nice turkey when they arrived.

His friends were not hunters and regarded him in a special way: a rough and tumble woodsman who could take care of himself in the wilderness, someone capable of bringing meat to the table without going to the grocery store—something they could never do. They'd be quite impressed if he had a wild turkey roasting in the oven when they arrived, and he envisioned the high-fives and good-natured backslapping he'd receive if he managed to pull it off. But he wasn't so sure he could. Unlike the fall season when any turkey was fair game, only bearded birds were legal in spring, which, for the most part, meant no hens. And worse yet, you could only hunt them by calling.

Well, that wasn't going to happen. The last time he tried to use a box call it sounded like nails on a chalkboard. Probably scared off half the birds in the county. No, he'd do it his way today. Besides, who would know? Certainly not his friends. The only seasons they knew anything about were baseball, football and basketball.

But luck was with him today, for he only walked a half mile when a turkey took wing just ahead. He shouldered his gun instantly. No time to waste—in seconds, it would be out of range. A quick point-and-shoot was all it took for the three-inch Remington number four shot to drop the bird like a lead weight.

An hour passed. The warden had been calling occasionally; a receptive gobbler had even answered once. But the woods had again grown silent, which was perfectly fine with him anyway. He tilted his head to the heavens. A blanket of high cirrus clouds containing millions of tiny ice crystals covered the sky, the light reflecting off the crystals creating a spectacular golden halo around the sun. A sight to behold, he thought, and a sure sign of rain (ring around the sun means rain to come). It was as good a time as any to head back down the mountain.

He was about to pack it in when a shotgun blast came from below. It was close, and the warden never heard anyone using a call. He took an orange ball cap from his back pocket and covered his head. Then he walked to the edge of the plateau where he saw a man dressed in camouflage a hundred yards away, and he started walking toward him.

As the poacher reached down to pick up his turkey, he heard someone approaching from behind and turned to see a hunter coming toward him through the woods.

"What do you have there?" called the hunter.

"It's a jake," said the poacher, tucking the bird under his arm. Then, turning quickly, he began to walk away.

"That doesn't look like a jake to me!"

There was an undertone of authority in the voice that caused the poacher to stop dead in his tracks and face him. There was something about the way the man carried himself that gave him pause. This was not the casual approach of a nosy hunter wanting to see his kill. The man strode toward him in long, vigorous steps, chin in the air, eyes clear and blazing with resolve. And when he reached him, he extracted a badge from his pocket. "State Game Warden," he said. "Hand me your shotgun."

The poacher complied, and the warden took it from him and ejected the remaining shells. Then he nodded at the turkey. "That's not a legal bird," he said.

"I know," admitted the poacher. "I thought I saw a beard when I shot it. It was an honest mistake. That's all."

"Where's your turkey call?"

The poacher checked his jacket pockets, digging into each one feverishly. "I don't know what happened to it," he said, feigning surprise. "I must have dropped it someplace."

The warden shook his head with open disbelief. "I see you haven't tagged the bird, either. That's another violation."

"But it's a mistake kill!" insisted the poacher. "I was gonna turn it in, so why tag it?"

"Because that's the law; you should try reading it once in a while."

The poacher swallowed hard and looked away. "I guess you're going to make me pay a fine, huh?"

"That's right," said the warden. "I want you to head down to my truck with me."

They descended mountain together in silence. When they reached the base, the warden put the illegal turkey in the bed of his pickup and walked around to the cab for a citation pad.

"How much is the fine?" asked the poacher.

"Three hundred dollars. You'll probably lose your hunting license for a year, too."

"You serious? For one turkey! Dude, that's pretty heavy!"

"One, you say? Let's take a look."

The warden dropped his tailgate and flipped the turkey on its back. Taking a small folding knife from his pocket, he carefully slit open its belly. Then, reaching inside the bird, he extracted twelve perfect eggs, one by one, and set them gently on the bed of his truck.

Published September 1997

You may go into the fields or down the lane, but don't go into Mr. McGregor's garden; your Father had an accident there; he was put in a pie by Mrs. McGregor.
~Beatrix Potter
The Tale of Peter Rabbit

Beauford

"**L**OOK! THERE'S A BUNNY OUTSIDE!**" cried my five-year-old daughter, Sarah. She was staring out the kitchen window, beaming with joy.

I walked over and stood behind her, then watched as the voracious cottontail devoured the last sprig of a firebush plant still peeking above the snowline.

That rabbit has got to go! I thought to myself. Then I looked down at my daughter's smiling face. How could I do that to her?

I felt like a real scrooge. What's one lousy plant anyway? I could always buy another one. After all, my daughter's happiness was at stake.

But that was two weeks ago. And as I stared out the kitchen window with my shoulders drooped in despair, my wife, Maryann, stepped over beside me.

"What are you looking at?" she asked.

"It looks like a brush hog has been at my shrubs," I said, shaking my head wearily. "That rabbit has got to go."

"But what about the kids?" she said. "They love that little rabbit."

"Little!" I grunted. "Have you seen it lately? It's as big as a housecat! Our firebush plants are gone. Eaten alive by that…that overgrown powderpuff!"

"But he's hungry. Besides, it's cold outside, and look at all the snow! The poor little guy has to eat *something*."

"Speaking of snow, do you see the drag mark between those foot prints? That's its belly! I've never seen a rabbit that big. The fact that it can still hop defies all science and reason."

"But he's so cute," insisted my wife.

"Cute!" I scoffed. "He looks like a bloated tick with fur!"

Maryann eyed me cautiously. "What are you planning to do, Bill? The kids will be very upset if you hurt him."

"I don't know. I could always set a box trap, take him someplace—"

"Hi Mom, hi Dad," said my eleven-year-old son, Jesse, as he walked into the kitchen. "Have you seen Beauford today?"

"Who's Beauford?" I asked.

"Beauford-the-bunny-rabbit, Dad. We named him, didn't you know?"

"Actually, I have a few names of my own, but I'll keep them to myself," I said. Then, more seriously: "Jesse, I'm going to take the rabbit someplace else, find him a new home. He's destroying our plants, and I'm afraid he might start girdling some of our trees and kill them."

Jesse looked up at me in wide-eyed disbelief. "Gee, Dad, do you have to?"

"Afraid so Jess, but I'll find a nice place for him to live. I promise."

And as I watched my son's expression change from disappointment to utter despair, I felt like the worst father in the whole world.

My wife put a hand on his shoulder and rubbed it gently. "It's okay, Jesse," she said softly. "Dad will find a nice new home for Beauford where he'll be happy."

Later that night, I was awakened by a strange noise coming from the back of the house. An erratic crunching sound, like someone chewing on crushed ice. I got out of bed, tiptoed down the hallway, and peered into the darkened kitchen. Moonlight streamed through a single window, highlighting the dim silhouette of a rabbit sitting on a chair by the dinner table. A rather large rabbit I might add. It was nibbling on the woody stalk of a firebush plant, its cheeks moving up-and-down in short, rapid strokes. It looked up at me and swallowed noisily. *Hi Bill, I'm Beauford,* it said. The voice, clear as day, was male, and it seemed to come from nowhere and everywhere at the same time.

"Wait a minute!" I blurted. "Is this a dream?"

Of course it is, bonehead! Rabbits can't talk!

I shook my head in disbelief. "What are you doing here?" I said. Then thought, good grief! Now I'm talking to a rabbit!

You don't really want to make your kids cry, do ya? he asked. *If you take me away, you'll break their little hearts.*

"But you're eating all my shrubs," I complained. "I protect birds and animals from poachers. Aren't rabbits supposed to like me? It just doesn't seem fair!"

C'mon Bill, Get a grip. You sound pathetic. Your shrubs will grow back bigger and better than ever come spring. Besides, they hadn't been pruned in years, and that's not too smart.

"Oh yeah!" I snorted. "Rabbits aren't exactly known for their intelligence you know!"

My point exactly.

"Huh?"

You're right. Rabbits aren't so smart. So rather than take me away and upset your litter...er, children...use that big hunk of gray matter upstairs to outwit me.

"How am I supposed to do that?"

Come here, he whispered.

I stepped close, then watched in awe as he arose, a shadow lifting like fog after a morning rain. He put a heavy hand (paw?) on my shoulder and gave me a nudge. *You don't really expect me to tell you that, do you...?*

"**B**ill, wake up!"

My eyes snapped open. It was my wife, her hand on my shoulder, shaking me. "You were talking in your sleep."

"Sorry," I breathed. "It was just a silly dream."

"It's three o'clock in the morning," she said softly. "Go back to sleep."

"Okay. You too."

But I didn't go back to sleep. Not for a long time. Instead, I lay on my back staring at the ceiling, trying to convince myself that it was only a dream. A dream that seemed all too real.

And so, over breakfast that morning, I told my family I decided not to take the rabbit away after all. "The shrubs needed a good pruning anyway," I reasoned. "And I'll wrap the trees with cloth so it can't girdle them."

"Did you decide that in your dream last night?" asked Maryann, needling me good-naturedly.

"Actually, it came to me as soon as I woke up this morning," I replied.

"You were mumbling something about talking rabbits," she said. "Going to tell us about it?"

"It was nothing, really," I insisted.

Suddenly my daughter cried, "Look! There's a bunny outside!" She was staring out the kitchen window in her teddy bear pajamas.

I walked over next to her and peered outside.

And there was Beauford, his furry cheeks busily grinding away on a tortured firebush. He seemed quite content. And because rabbits, like most prey species, have eyes on the sides of their head to watch for predators, I could only see the side that was facing me. So it may not have been a wink that I saw, but a blinking of both eyes simultaneously.

In any case, since that day, I've never spoken disparagingly about the rabbit again, and have taken to calling him Beauford just like the rest of my family.

<hr>

Published January 1993

41

In every age "the good old days" were a myth.
No one ever thought they were good at the time.
~Brooks Atkinson

The Good Old Days

RUMMAGING THROUGH A STACK of old hunting
magazines at a yard sale, I was surprised to find a tattered copy
of *Pennsylvania Game Laws* from 1915. I promptly purchased
it for twenty-five cents, a bargain to say the least. When I
opened the old leaflet, fragile and yellowed with age, I became
captivated by the similarities, as well as the differences, with
our present-day wildlife laws in Pennsylvania.

Contrary to our current five-day bear season, hunters could
pursue bears from mid-October to mid-December, and could
kill one bear per hunter or "three bears to one camp or body
of men." Today the limit is still one bear per hunter, but there
is no longer a camp limit. Bears were not as plentiful eighty
years ago, nor were there as many hunters as today, so a longer
season was needed to hunt them successfully. In 1915,
Pennsylvania hunters harvested 188 bears during the two-
month season. Compare that to the 2,598 bears killed in 1998,
with all of them taken in a matter of three days! To be sure,
bear hunting is better than ever in Pennsylvania.

Deer hunting was also very different in the early nineteen
hundreds. Does were completely protected by a closed season,
and hunters could take only bucks during the first two weeks
of December. The season limit was one deer per hunter, or
"six to one camp or body of men." There was no special
archery or muzzleloader season in those days, and in fact,

bows and arrows were illegal for deer hunting. Today our modern deer seasons run from early September into January, with an additional special extended season for farms experiencing deer damage. In 1915, Pennsylvania hunters harvested just over 1,300 deer; today the harvest approaches, and sometimes exceeds, 400,000 whitetails annually.

The names of certain game species were different in those days, too. Quail, for instance, were known as Virginia partridge. Ruffed grouse (our state bird) were called pheasants. Our common walleye was dubbed either pike-perch or Susquehanna salmon, and bobcats were known as wild-cats.

In 1915, hunters could shoot "web-footed wild water fowl" from mid-September through the end of January in unlimited numbers, and it was legal to sell waterfowl to restaurants during open hunting seasons. Today both state and federal laws protect waterfowl from market hunting and over-harvest by setting reasonable bag limits for hunters, and our waterfowl seasons usually last one month instead of almost four.

What surprised me most about our game and fish laws in 1915 was the endless list of birds and animals that were unprotected, most of them because they killed game species. The following could be killed year round without a hunting license (which cost one dollar): blue jays, kingfishers, buzzards, goshawks, sharp-shinned hawks, cooper's hawks, red-tailed hawks, red-shouldered hawks, broad-winged hawks, marsh hawks, rough-legged hawks, duck hawks, pigeon hawks, barrel owls, great gray owls, great horned owls, snowy owls, northern hawk-owls, ravens, crows, great blue herons, green herons, night herons, opossums, woodchucks, bobcats, foxes, mink, weasels, muskrats, and skunks.

Interestingly, the duck hawk listed above is now an endangered species, but hunting alone did not bring on its decline. Residue from the chemical known as DDT (now banned), widely used as a pesticide after World War II, washed into our waterways where plants and fish absorbed it into their skins. Fish-eating ducks ingested this residue when they consumed the contaminated fish, and duck hawks (now called peregrine falcons) became affected after preying on these ducks. Many hawks died, and those that lived began to lay thin-shelled eggs that wouldn't hatch, causing the population to decline drastically. Bald eagles were similarly affected as they prey largely on fish. Today, thanks to modern conservation practices, both peregrine falcons and bald eagles have made a dramatic comeback nationwide.

In 1915, bounties were paid for what Pennsylvania considered to be the leading game killers, with a six-dollar reward for bobcats, two dollars for fox, and a dollar for each weasel or mink killed. Bounties were dropped on bobcats and weasels in 1938 due to a significant decline in numbers, but the bounty on red and gray foxes was increased to four dollars and a five-dollar bounty on great horned owls was introduced. Pennsylvania started its bounty system back in 1683, paying rewards on wolves, cougars, squirrels, foxes, mink, weasels and all species of hawks and owls. The bounty system continued for almost three-hundred years until it ceased in 1966.

The Pennsylvania Game Commission has gone through many changes in its history. But it has come a long way in the last hundred years, creating one of the best wildlife management programs in the nation. Most game animals are more plentiful than ever, and the agency has developed sound strategies that have brought back our eagles, ospreys, peregrine falcons, beavers, bobcats, otters, and other animals of concern.

Hunters and trappers paid for these programs over the years through the purchase of hunting and furtaking licenses. Which brings this thought to mind: Maybe the folks who are running around hugging trees and polar bears these days ought to be hugging hunters instead. Because not only are they paying for our wildlife, but also, unlike trees and bears, they just might hug you back.

Published May 1998

44

A feeling of sadness comes o'er me that my soul cannot resist
And resembles sorrow only, as the mist resembles the rain.
~Henry Wadsworth Longfellow

In The Line of Duty

November 7, 1915

Indian summer had come late that year as Joseph McHugh strolled down the railroad tracks enjoying the fresh, earthy smells of the neighboring fields and woodlands. The sun was shining brightly, and many trees still bore their colorful autumn foliage. A crimson leaf drifted lazily by in the warm breeze and he reached out and caught it. He held it in the palm of his hand, tracing each tiny vein with a fingertip as he marveled at God's creation. He loved all things wild, and though he was happy to be alive on such a beautiful fall day, Joseph McHugh, a Pennsylvania Game Protector for less than six months, was about to die.

It was no accident he was here, for there had been reports of unlawful hunting over the past few weeks. And although he hadn't heard any gunshots thus far, he thought he'd make the most of the lovely weather and amble on for a while rather than return home to an empty house (the wife and kids were off to grandma's). The day was just too pretty to waste.

Rounding a bend in the railroad, he unexpectedly bumped into an old friend, William Brown, who'd been out looking for his dog, Trusty. They continued down the tracks together, hoping they'd soon find Brown's pet. As they walked, the two men chatted about their younger days, with the conversation turning to the time when Brown had snuck a shoebox full of

45

mice into Mrs. Dawkins schoolhouse and dumped them on the floor while she was busy at the blackboard. The girls all stood on their chairs screaming like banshees, and Mrs. Dawkins was forced to cancel class and send everyone home early.

They both laughed out loud as they thought back on it. Then Brown reminded McHugh that he'd won the bet on who would catch the biggest fish later that afternoon.

"Is that right?" said McHugh. "I don't remember that at all."

Brown nodded appreciatively. "So I guess you don't remember the quarter you owe me on our wager, either."

"Quarter! I thought it was a penny!"

"And I thought you didn't remember."

"Okay. You got me," chuckled McHugh. He dug into his pockets, fished around for some change, and shrugged meekly. "Looks like you'll have to wait until tomorrow."

Brown shook his head and smiled good-naturedly. "Been waiting thirty years, my friend. Guess I can wait a little longer."

"But it was a penny, not a quarter," insisted McHugh.

"Yes, I know, but I'm charging interest."

"Interest!"

"Yep. But I'll tell you what: if you help me find Trusty today, I'll not only relieve you of your debt, I'll cook you a nice dinner tonight. How's that?"

"Sure about that?"

"Word of honor."

McHugh cupped a hand to his mouth and turned toward the open fields bordering the tracks. "HEEEEEERE, TRUSTY! C'MON BOY. BROWNIE'S COOKING STEAKS TONIGHT!"

"Steaks?" grunted Brown. "I didn't say anything about steaks!"

McHugh turned to him and grinned. "I like mine medium rare."

The two men walked the tracks for another mile with no sign of Brown's dog. Along the way, McHugh talked about his new calling. It was no secret that his recent position with the Pennsylvania Game Commission had been a major job change. At age forty, he'd left Prudential as a successful insurance salesman to begin his career as a state game protector. It was a big adjustment in his life, but he knew it was the right move. He loved hunting and the outdoors, and this new opportunity was a dream come true.

As he was sharing these feelings with Brown, they heard the sudden frenzied baying of hounds behind a distant railroad tower, and McHugh suspected that poaching activity was afoot. Hunting on Sunday was illegal (the fine, ten dollars), so both men quickly descended the tracks and began working their way across a broad meadow toward the wailing hounds.

They soon encountered a man carrying a shotgun. He had a circle of dogs with him. McHugh, who was wearing civilian clothes, (officers did not have uniforms in those days), asked if he'd had any luck.

"Just gettin' started," the hunter said.

"Where are you from?" asked McHugh.

The man eyed him suspiciously. "Drifton," he said.

"Nice bunch of dogs; are they all yours?"

"Nope. Why?"

McHugh offered an easy shrug. "Just that it's a lot of dogs for one person to handle."

"Most of them belong to my friends. There's five of us."

McHugh nodded and smiled amiably. "What about your friends? Anybody else have luck?"

The hunter's eyes cut left and right, then narrowed sharply. "You ask a lot of questions, mister. How come?"

McHugh pulled a badge from his pocket and identified himself. "I'm a state game protector, son. I want you to unload your gun."

The man never gave him a chance. In an abrupt and reckless move, he pointed his shotgun at the lawman and pulled the trigger, the blast from the twenty-gauge slamming into his chest like a ton of bricks.

McHugh stared unbelievingly into the man's face, then fell to the ground fatally wounded. There was no pain, just a great, surging numbness. And he thought of his wife, Isabella, and their three children ages four, six, and eight. What would they do without him?

Then darkness overtook him, and he was gone.

The poacher immediately turned his gun on Brown. "Put your hands up!"

Brown raised both hands and took an impulsive step back.

"DON'T MOVE!" the poacher shouted. "You stay right there!" He glared at him with the cold, unblinking eyes of a serpent as he snapped open his hinge-action shotgun and extracted a smoking shell. The man intended to execute Brown and wanted him to stand there like a doomed prisoner at a firing squad waiting to be cut down.

As the poacher took a live round from his pocket to reload, Brown took another step back.

"Hey!" the poacher barked. "Where do you think you're going?" Then he pushed the shell into the breach of his shotgun and snapped it closed.

Brown froze, his stomach wrenching into a sharp knot as he closed his eyes and waited for the terrible blast to come.

The poacher pointed the barrel at Brown's chest, pulled back the hammer, and then calmly pulled the trigger… *Click!*

Brown jerked back reflexively from the impact that never came, then quickly opened his eyes only to see the poacher pull back the hammer once again. Brown stared at the deadly muzzle, big as a cannon, and took another step back.

The poacher squeezed the trigger again, and again it failed, encouraging Brown to turn quickly and start walking away.

Seconds became minutes as Brown waited for the blast that would send him sprawling to the ground.

He glanced over his shoulder. The poacher had his head down, fidgeting with the gun, unaware that he was slipping away.

So he ran. Ran for his life. And when he chanced a look back, the poacher was gone...

October 3, 1995

And so some eighty years later, thirty uniformed game wardens stand ceremoniously in a cold autumn rain at a memorial service dedicated to Joseph J. McHugh and his family.

We stand in attention by his grave in two columns and watch fellow officers place a wreath as a cold rain envelops us. We stand in solemn detail as our fallen comrade is honored by a twenty-one-gun salute. And a boy plays taps at his graveside.

It was a moving experience that day at a tiny church in rural Pennsylvania. One officer later told me he thought the rain was quite appropriate for it added to the somber mood of the men.

I couldn't agree more. And although for the most part the rain had been cold and raw, I remember feeling a warm drop trickle slowly down my face as I stood by his grave with my men.

Published October 1995

Author's Note:

Ninety-five years later, almost to the day, after Joseph McHugh was fatally shot, Pennsylvania Wildlife Conservation Officer David L. Grove was murdered by a deer poacher in Adams County. He was thirty-one, and had been a game warden for less than three years when his life was taken. As in the McHugh case, there was an eyewitness present during the shooting—a passenger riding in the poacher's truck—who watched the poacher gun down the warden as he

49

attempted to arrest him for unlawfully killing a deer at night. The poacher emptied his forty-five caliber handgun and reloaded at least once during the intense twenty-five-shot gunfight with the officer. Grove managed to wound him before being fatally wounded himself.

Unlike the McHugh case, where the suspect was found not guilty (two top defense attorneys managed to convince a jury that the poacher acted in self-defense), David Grove's killer was convicted and sentenced to die by lethal injection.

Since the first known deaths in 1886, two hundred and ninety game wardens from sixty-five different state agencies have been killed in the line of duty.

Give me your arm, old toad;
Help me down Cemetery Road.
 ~Phillip Larkin

Bones

LYING THERE, BREATHING IN LABORED shallow gasps, he appeared close to death. I was driving along a rugged two-track dirt lane in a remote part of the county when I happened to look to my left. The dog was starving. Ribs pushing against his coat as if about to burst through. A crooked line of blood trickled from his right eye. The left one bulged in its socket, lifeless and gray. He was under a large multiflora rose bush, the warm September sun hammering on his wasted body.

I exited my patrol car and slowly approached. Rabies had reared its ugly head earlier in the summer. Perhaps the dog was stricken. I had killed a number of sick raccoons and foxes in past weeks, submitting their heads to the state lab for analysis. Most had come back positive. I stepped closer, examining the emaciated dog with my eyes. An adult coonhound, medium-sized, white with brown spots. Although obviously someone's pet, he wore no collar.

There was an overwhelming look of helplessness about the dog, as if he had finally given up. He lay on his side, his tortured head resting on the ground as he watched me with his one good eye. Had it not been for the faint swell of his chest, you might think he was dead. And I thought grimly that he was fortunate in a sorrowful way, for his agony would soon end. Had I not happened by, he would have suffered horribly for another day or more.

Saddened by the thought that death was so near, I knelt by his side. "Easy, fella," I whispered. I placed my hand gently upon his chest. He trembled briefly at my touch, then his boney tail, curled between his legs, began to move from side to side. Encouraged, I stayed with him, stroking his head and telling him everything would be okay. And as I did this, his breathing began to grow stronger, more regular. And suddenly I had hope for him.

I returned to my patrol car and radioed Wyoming County Communications, informing the dispatcher that I was in a field just off Cemetery Road with a severely emaciated dog in need of attention. The dispatcher made several phone calls, and within minutes, two Humane Society agents were in route.

I hung up my mic, walked back to the dog, and briskly stroked his head. "I'll be back," I said. Then I climbed into my patrol car and drove a short distance to a roadside mountain stream. I grabbed my empty thermos and filled it with cold, refreshing water. It would be just what he needed to help him feel better. Returning to the dog, I kneeled by him. His tail began to wag as I unscrewed the thermos lid and filled it with water. I lowered it to his face and he lapped it eagerly, his long tongue curling into the cup seeking every last drop.

"Easy, boy," I said, pulling the cup away. "I have more."

I refilled the lid two more times and watched him lap it dry. "That's good for now, fella," I cautioned. "Drink too much and you'll get sick."

He seemed to understand, and so I sat there with his head on my lap, kneading his scalp with my fingers while waiting for help to arrive.

But the humane agents were a considerable distance away, and I remembered seeing a house nearby where I might get something for him to eat before they arrived. I stood to leave, and he looked up at me and moaned softly.

"Gotta go, buddy," I said. "But I'll be back soon. Promise."

I got into my patrol car and followed the two-track out to Cemetery Road. Turning right, I soon came to a farmhouse with a collie tied under a maple tree out front. I pulled into the driveway and parked, figuring they'd likely have some dog food on hand.

As I approached the front door, a woman stepped out to greet me. She was in her fifties, dressed in jeans and a flannel shirt, her skin tanned and weathered from years of toil in the sun.

"Game warden!" she said nervously. "I hope my men aren't in any trouble."

"No, ma'am," I said. "I was hoping you could help me. I found an injured coonhound not far from here. Any idea who might own him?"

"Coon hound, you say?"

"Yes. He's white and brown."

She folded her arms across her broad chest and thought for a moment. "Can't say that I do," she said. "If there was any coon hunting going on around here I'd hear the dogs bellowing like all get-out. They make quite a fuss you know."

"Yes, ma'am."

"You sure it's a coonhound?"

I nodded.

With that, she turned and hollered toward the barn. "Yoo-hoo! Daniel! Come on out here please." She looked at me and nodded confidently. "My husband might know something."

A man dressed in faded coveralls and a worn flannel shirt came from the barn and walked over to greet me. "Game warden!" he exclaimed, offering a calloused hand. "How can I help ya?" He had a booming voice, and spoke as if I were a hundred feet away instead of right in front of him.

His wife chimed in before I had a chance: "Somebody lost a coonhound, Daniel," she said. "Know anybody who owns a coonhound? The officer says he's white and brown."

"I found him about a quarter mile from here," I said. "He's in bad shape."

"That's too bad," said Daniel. "They nice dogs. Real nice dogs. But nobody around here owns one."

I handed him a calling card with my name and phone number. "If anyone comes looking for the dog, give me a call, okay?"

He took the card and stuffed it into his pocket. "I'll do that officer. I surely will."

I thanked them and asked if I could have some dog food to take with me.

"Why of course you can dear," the woman said. "Wait right here and I'll go inside and get some for you."

She walked back to the house and soon returned with a lunch bag filled to the brim.

"Don't give him too much at first," she said. "He might throw up."

W hen I returned for the dog, I was shocked to see he was gone. I called for him, noting the alarm in my own voice. Suddenly I saw him. He had moved fifteen yards to lie under the shade of a larger multiflora rose bush. That he was able to do this was truly a promising sign.

I went over to him and kneeled by his side. "Hey, fella; told you I'd be back." I shook the bag of food and held it out to him. "Look what I brought!"

His tail thumped the ground as I took a nugget from the bag and offered it, and he quickly whisked the morsel from my palm with his tongue and chewed. I dipped into the bag again, taking a handful this time, and held the nourishment under his chin with cupped palms. He bored into the food with his muzzle, chewing ravenously. When he finished, I gave him another drink of water and massaged his floppy ears with my fingers.

"Feel better now?" I asked. He inched closer and nestled his head on my lap. Then he closed his eyes and I held him there for a while, watching the rhythmic rise and fall of his chest.

Suddenly my two-way radio came alive: *"Wyoming County to five-three-eight!"*

It was police dispatcher Brad Killian. I raised my portable radio to my face and keyed the mic. "Five-three-eight by."

"Animal rescue is coming up Cemetery Road now. Can you meet them?"

"Ten-four," I replied. "Have them stand by. I'll drive out there now."

The county agent, Karen Killian, gasped when I drove her back to the dog and she saw his wretched condition. We walked over and knelt by him, speaking softly and petting his head before lifting him to his feet. And when he stood, although a bit wobbly-legged, he wagged his boney tail for us.

Karen said the other agent would be along in a few minutes and that she'd be driving a county owned van sufficiently equipped to transport the dog to a veterinary clinic. Karen had come in her personal car, which was all she had available at the time. I handed her my portable radio in case she needed to contact me and drove back to meet the other agent.

The van was parked along Cemetery Road when I arrived. I thanked the agent for coming and was about transport her back in my patrol car when Karen called on my radio explaining that she had started walking the dog out but he stopped after fifty feet, too weak to walk any farther. Fortunately, the county agent's van was equipped with a stretcher, so I put it in my vehicle and drove back to meet Karen.

The coonhound was lying on his side when I got there, so I set the stretcher beside him, and with Karen's help, laid him gently on the canvas bed. Then we each took one end of the stretcher and carried him back to Cemetery road where we loaded him ever so carefully into the county van.

From there he was transported to the Tunkhannock Veterinary Clinic where it was determined he had tangled with a porcupine. One fateful quill had pierced his left eye, permanently blinding him. Dozens of others had worked their way so deeply into his face and neck they were no longer visible above the skin. Each quill was painstakingly removed at the clinic, were he was treated for dehydration and severe emaciation as well.

I stopped by to see him later in the week. He looked much better, and I reached out and massaged his floppy ears one final time. Soft and warm.

The folks at the clinic named him Bones. Appropriate to say the least. And lest you think this story doesn't have a happy ending, I'm pleased to report that a family of four adopted Bones from the clinic shortly after his recovery.

———————————————
Published September 1997

Thou call'dst me dog before thou hadst a cause,
But, since I am a dog, beware my fangs.
    ~Shakespeare

Winter Kill

WITH HER FAT RESERVES NEARLY DEPLETED,
she could feel her strength draining. The long, harsh winter
had taken its toll. Instinct told her to be still. Her energy must
be conserved if she were to survive.

The others were gone. But it was not hunger or cold that
killed them. One by one they had journeyed into the
snowfields in search of food. Then the dogs would come. Well
fed, swift and nimble, they would overtake them, gaping jaws
slashing and tearing at their flanks until exhausted they would
fall.

She rarely left the conifer stands. The dense pines blocked
the cold north winds and absorbed heat from the sun during
the day. And that, combined with her heavy coat with its
hollow hairs, enabled her to bed comfortably in the snow.
There was little to eat there, and she had lost thirty percent of
her body mass since summer, but the pines offered a safe and
peaceful solitude that kept her at ease.

The winter had been brutal, but as the days grew longer and
the sun warmer she sensed its end was near—and with it, an
end to the hardship and hunger.

And so she survived day by day, venturing from the pines
to browse on stems of maple and beech only when the pangs
of hunger forced her. If the dogs came for her, she would flee.
And though the deep snows and lack of food had surely taken

their toll, her pregnancy had compounded her dwindling stamina all the more, so even if she eluded them, untouched by their fangs, the physical exertion alone might kill her.

The man who lived at the edge of the snowfields was a good husband and a good father. He worked hard every day to provide for his wife and twin sons. He was a carpenter by trade, specializing in home building. But the long winter and poor economy had forced him from his job. Construction projects within a hundred mile radius had all but stopped, so he stayed home most days. Alone.

His wife, a nurse, worked at the local hospital, and both children were in fifth grade with Mrs. Hopkins. So the man had only his dogs for company during the day. And although he was alone he was never lonely, thanks to his two faithful companions.

Both dogs were well-muscled black and tan mongrels with powerful legs and broad chests, courtesy of their Rottweiler and German shepherd ancestry. They were well cared for and adored. Their licenses were renewed on time each year and their rabies shots kept up to date. He even took them to the veterinarian clinic for general check-ups on a regular basis, which was more than he did for himself. They barked when strangers knocked, played well with the children, and enjoyed curling by their master's feet as he sat in his favorite chair watching TV or reading the newspaper. They always obeyed his commands and they never had accidents in the house.

Yes, they were good dogs. Very good dogs indeed.

Every evening after supper, after the kids had finished their homework and gone to bed, he would let his dogs out for a run. But tonight they would have to wait as he sat with his wife in the den by a warm fire and listened to her talk about her day. She had a demanding position in the hospital that kept her on her feet attending to patients throughout her ten-hour shift. Their lives depended on her, but no matter how hard she tried, she couldn't save them all. And today had been one of those days. He held her hand and he listened, comforting her through her tears. He reminded her of all the people whose lives she had changed for the better, people who'd gained strength through the comfort of her smiles and attentive care, people who had called her their guardian angel. And gradually, lovingly, he brought her back.

And when exhausted she went to bed, he sat staring at the fire, struggling with that nagging twinge of envy that tugged at his conscience, that empty feeling of discontent knowing that his wife had purpose and usefulness in her life while he sat home day after day.

But when his dogs jumped up and ran to the door, his mood suddenly brightened. Didn't they depend on him as much as any patient depends on his nurse? Of course they did! And it was time to let them run. After all, they needed their exercise just as the sick needed to rise from their beds to get their tired blood circulating.

He arose from his recliner as they whined and danced by the door. And like always, he released them into the night, the full moon casting a silver sheen on the snow as they dashed into the surrounding darkness.

The good dogs charged across the snowfields until they came to the frozen remains of a deer carcass. They circled it, each lifting a leg to mark their territory. It had been many days since they had killed, and the urge to hunt was keen. And so, with heads raised into the wind, they began to search for pleasant scents.

Bedded down for the night, she was alone but not lonely, for she could sense the twin fawns growing in her belly. She lay in a depression in the snow, hungry but content within the shelter of the pines. And had it not been for the approaching storm she would have gone undetected. But with it came an early wind. A wind that carried her scent far into the bleak snowfields that surrounded her.

Alerted to her presence, they advanced in deadly silence. And thus, she never heard them until they were upon her. She bolted from her bed and sprinted through the snow, her long and graceful legs plunging through the crust with every footfall, impeding her escape.

But the dogs, lighter and wide of foot, ran easily atop the compacted snow. They paced themselves, tongues lolling from gaping jaws as they followed her. And for every step she made, her pursuers traveled three.

They could smell her fear. They sensed her growing fatigue. Tasted her flesh.

She could hear them gaining on her, their deadly pads slapping the snowpack in an even, measured gait, the low growls ushered from their throats, the steady cadence of their breathing.

The good dogs caught her easily.

They dragged her down, wild-eyed and frantic.

And she was gone.

W ithin the past three weeks, the Game Commission's northeast region office received thirty complaints of dogs attacking deer. District game wardens have confirmed each case. Eight complaints were in Wyoming County alone. Unfortunately, this was probably a small percentage of actual incidents.

The penalty is substantial, up to five hundred dollars per dog. Furthermore, the Game and Wildlife Code permits dogs attacking deer to be destroyed.

Ironically, I was called about a pack of dogs chasing a deer while writing this article. They had the deer down twice and are still after her. Deputy Gene Gaydos is on his way out there now...

Published January 1994

Somebody just back of you while you are fishing is as bad as someone looking over your shoulder while you write a letter to your girl.
~Ernest Hemingway

Over the Limit

AFTER STOCKING THE CREEK with several hundred lively trout, the warden stashed his vehicle a quarter-mile away and returned dressed in camouflage fatigues. Poaching had become more frequent here, so he concealed himself behind a laurel thicket fifty yards from the streambank and waited.

Trout season was open, and because he had chosen a popular spot with local anglers, it wasn't long before a battered old pickup truck came rattling down the graveled township road and parked a few yards from the water. A portly man in his mid-thirties exited the vehicle trailed by a woman of similar age and proportions. They walked to the stream's edge and peered into the crystal water, the man scratching his heavy beard vigorously while his woman stood quietly at his side.

"Looks like they dumped a ton of fish in here, Annie," he said. "You can see 'em swimming around!"

She nodded in agreement. "I'll bet they'll be biting good, too," she said. "Let's go back and get the kids so we can catch more fish."

"Good idea," said the bearded man. "If we hurry, we'll have the whole place to ourselves." And with that intriguing thought in mind, they climbed into their pickup truck and sped back down the road toward home.

The warden had been squatting low where the laurels were thickest so he wouldn't be discovered. He stood now to stretch his legs. There would be plenty of time to hunker down again when the truck returned; he'd hear it coming long before it came into view. He dug into his jacket pocket, pulled out a peanut butter sandwich and tore it from its plastic wrapper. It was chunky on white bread, his favorite. He took a healthy bite and chewed, the crunchy, peanutty taste causing his empty stomach to purr like a kitten. The only thing missing was a cold glass of milk to go with it, he thought. But he'd left his thermos behind.

Trout season had kept him working practically around the clock for the weeks. The days had been crazy with complaints of anglers trespassing on private property and taking over the limit of fish. With six hundred square miles to cover, it had been difficult to be everywhere at once, but that's what everyone seemed to expect of him, including his boss.

No sooner had he finished his sandwich, when he heard a distant backfire followed by the erratic putt and rumble of a vehicle chugging down the road. He quickly dropped into a squat behind the laurels and watched as the pickup truck returned. The bearded man sat behind the wheel, his woman at the passenger side while two teenaged children, a girl and a boy, sat tight between them. The truck grunted and squeaked on worn springs as it pulled past him and parked by the edge of the creek.

The bearded man was first to climb out. "C'mon Annie!" he called. "We ain't got all day!"

Annie opened the passenger door and walked to the rear of the truck with her children. She unlatched the tailgate and dropped it with a clang, then reached into the bed to gather equipment for everyone.

The bearded man, anxious to get started, squeezed by her and grabbed his fishing rod and bait first.

"Don't be a hog!" she snapped at him. "We want to catch fish just as bad as you do!"

He grunted at her and stormed off, his rod in one hand and a can of worms in the other.

Annie shook her head wearily and faced her children. "Promise me you won't grow up to be a grouch like your father," she said.

They said nothing. Instead, they dutifully took their fishing rods and bait cans from her, the daughter moving downstream with her father while the son stayed with his mother.

The warden watched through binoculars as they cast their lines into the shimmering water. He was behind them, a stone's throw away, and could hear every word they said.

The bearded man and his daughter didn't talk at all. But the mother spoke nonstop to her sixteen-year-old son, Bobby, who could care less, as it was mostly gossip about her neighbors. Bobby cast his line upstream barely glancing at his mother as she prattled on. He let his line drift with the current until it floated twenty yards or so downstream, then reeled in and checked his bait before casting upstream again. He did this repeatedly and soon had a bite.

"Got one!" he cried.

All heads turned as he jerked back the tip of his rod and set the hook. Still lively from the cold mountain water, the rainbow trout fought hard, jumping and splashing vigorously until the boy brought it ashore.

After dislodging the hook from its mouth, he threw the fish toward his mother who was fishing about ten feet away from him. It landed beside her, flopping helplessly on the stony shore.

"Nice one, Bobby!" she declared. Then she picked up the trout and dropped it into a five-gallon plastic bucket by her side.

Bobby smiled proudly as he put a fresh worm on his hook, leaving a third of its squirming body dangling below the barb for eye appeal. He cast his line upstream, and within seconds caught another trout and tossed it toward his mother. As she scooped it up, her daughter suddenly hooked a trout of her own and began to reel it in. When she got it to the bank, she raised her rod straight up, allowing the trout to dangle in front of her face, its gleaming body jerking and thrashing as if an electric current ran through it.

"Ewwwww!" she cried. "I don't want to touch it!"

Her father glanced over at her and scowled, then continued to fish a few feet away. "Annie, give her a hand with the fish!" he bellowed over his shoulder.

Annie waddled over to her daughter and removed the trout from her line. "Want me to bait your hook for you, too?" she sneered. "Don't be such a sissy!"

Then as she walked back to her spot, a baby began to cry inside the pickup truck. Annie never so much as glanced its way. Instead, she lit a cigarette, picked up her rod, and cast her line into the water with her back turned to the child, its squalling growing more intense by the second.

The warden clenched his jaw, uncertain how much longer he'd let the infant cry before stepping in. He had two young children of his own, and it ate at his guts to hear the baby screaming. But after a minute or so, Annie pitched her cigarette into the water, put down her rod, and started up the bank toward the truck. "I'm coming," she called. "Hold your water, baby girl. Mama's coming."

The warden continued to watch as they cast their lines into the current, allowing their baited hooks to drift and bounce off the rocky bottom before casting out once again. But he was caught off guard when the boy suddenly reeled in his line and started walking away with his fishing rod.

"Where do you think you're going, Bobby?" called his mother.

"I ain't catching nothing here," he said. "I'm gonna head upstream."

"You best stay put, son," she warned. "I don't have a license, and you'll need to take my rod if the game warden comes by. I don't want no ticket!"

"But I ain't catching nothing, Mom!"

"Put a fresh worm on, Bobby. A nice lively one! Yours is plumb drowned by now."

Bobby plodded over to his mother and took a fat nightcrawler from her bait can. It thrashed and squirmed as he pushed his hook into its segmented body.

"Why are you taking one of *my* worms?" his mother protested. "I don't have that many!"

"'Cause yours are bigger," snickered Bobby. But his amusement was abruptly cut short by an approaching vehicle, gravel cracking under its tires like popcorn. Thinking it might be the warden, Annie quickly dropped her rod and walked hurriedly toward her truck. She was halfway there when she saw that it was just a passing motorist making his way down the road. Relieved, she shuffled back down the bank to the shoreline and continued fishing next to her son.

The warden had been watching from the laurels for a good half hour and was about to step from the thicket when Bobby suddenly fell into a fishing frenzy, hooking one trout after another. His father and sister began catching trout too, and before long, their five-gallon bucket was half-full of fish.

Annie soon began to grow worried about all the trout her son was catching. "Bobby," she said. "You have sixteen fish already. Maybe we should go."

"Not yet Mom," insisted Bobby. "We can have twenty-four trout in that bucket and still be legal as long as nobody knows who caught them." He called to his sister downstream. "Wanna stick around sis? Catch a few more?"

She turned. Fifteen years old. A cigarette dangling from her lips. "Yeah. Let's stay. This is way cool!"

But before long, they had thirty trout in the bucket, and Bobby's mom grew more worried. "Bobby," she said insistently, "we have way over the limit. We're all gonna get tickets if we get caught."

"Don't worry, Mom," said Bobby. "We'll see the game warden's car long before he gets here. If we do, I'll run the bucket downstream and dump the fish in the rapids. He'll never know we caught a thing."

The warden now realized he'd have to wait until Bobby moved away from the illegal fish in order to secure the bucket for evidence. But his knees were beginning to cramp from squatting, and he didn't know how much longer he could stay crouched. He was about to take his chances and move quickly toward them when Bobby turned and started walking up the bank, away from the bucket. The warden didn't know what he was up to until he saw him duck behind a tree to relieve himself.

It was time to move. Advancing on stiffened legs, he stepped from the laurels and quickly descended the bank. Bobby heard him coming and whipped his head around, his face a mask of comic surprise. Caught in mid-stream, he couldn't move. "Mom!" he shouted. "The bucket! Dump the bucket!"

His mother looked over her shoulder and saw the advancing lawman. She dropped her gear and started for the bucket, but in her haste, tripped over her rod and fell facedown into the creek.

She floundered helplessly in the frigid water for several seconds before struggling to her knees. Unable to stand on her own, she blinked stupidly, gagging and spitting until finally catching her breath. "Oh my! Oh my!" she gasped. "I almost drowned!"

Her family rushed to her aid. It took all three to raise the gargantuan woman to her feet, her wet clothes clinging to her body as if spray-painted on.

"We're caught!" she puffed as they brought her from the water. "Oh mercy me, we're caught!"

The warden stood on the bank as they stumbled ashore, their eyes searching the ground in collective embarrassment, when her husband glanced at the bucket of fish. "Annie! For goodness' sake!" he exclaimed. "How many trout did you and Bobby catch?"

She glared at him through dripping curls of tangled hair and shook her head sadly. He knew Bobby had caught way over the limit, and now he wanted to play dumb.

She turned to the warden with frightened eyes. "It was me," she muttered woefully. "Bobby didn't do nothing wrong. I caught all the fish. You can take me to jail if you want, because it's all my doing, officer."

The warden couldn't help feeling a pang of sympathy for the woman, knowing she was only trying to protect her son. But he was old enough to know better, and he wasn't about to let him off the hook. "I appreciate what you're trying to do, ma'am, but I've been watching you for quite a while. Never saw you reel in a single fish. But your son caught twenty-three trout, and that's seventeen over the limit."

"You been spying on us warden?" the bearded man said acidly. "Pretty sneaky if you ask me."

The warden looked at Bobby. "So is catching over the limit of trout and dumping them into the creek when the game warden comes around."

Bobby shoved both hands into his pockets and bowed his head as the warden pulled a citation pad from his pocket and began writing citations for the illegal fish. When he finished, he sent them on their way, hoping they had all learned a lesson, as the fines were considerable.

The following day, the warden returned to the creek and was astonished to see Bobby fishing there again. He was alone this time, and the warden had no idea if his parents knew about it. He stood behind the laurels and watched him for a while. After thirty minutes and no bites, the boy attached a large weighted treble hook to his line and cast it into the creek. He did this repeatedly until he snagged a trout by its belly and brought the impaled fish ashore.

This time the warden didn't wait to see how many more trout he'd catch. He promptly stepped from the laurel thicket and stopped him before he could foul-hook another. Then he seized his fishing rod and ticketed him for poaching once again.

Incredibly, when the warden came back the next day and hid behind the laurels, Bobby and his father returned in their banged-up truck and pulled in by the creek. After exiting the vehicle, they walked up and down the bank searching feverishly for him, cursing him all the while. Satisfied he wasn't around to spy on them, they settled down and cast their lines into the water. But after thirty minutes with no bites, Bobby's father started packing up their gear.

"What are you doing, Dad?" asked Bobby.

"Place must've been cleaned out by all the fish hogs that come up from the city!" he muttered sourly. "Let's get out of here and find someplace else to fish."

And with that, they marched back to their truck, climbed inside, and stormed down the graveled country road in a cloud of brown dust.

Published July 1998

Who shall bell the cat?
     ~Aesop (500 B.C.)

Tiger

SHE SENSED A HIDDEN DANGER crouching just ahead, and so she remained motionless, her paralyzing fear turning her to stone save the faint tremble of her chest.

Her body tensed with anticipation. The woodchuck burrow just ahead was her only chance for escape. Whatever creature lay in wait would soon strike, for the soft summer breeze carried her scent directly to it.

She bolted, ears pressed against her head, eyes filled with terror as she raced toward the sanctuary of the yawning hollow, so close she could smell the clay soil that would usher her to safety. Mere seconds separated her from its refuge, the green grass a blur as she rocketed onward.

But the rabbit was up against a predator the likes of which she couldn't fathom. A super-killer. A plunderer of nestlings and newborns. With muscles taut as steel springs, he crouched. Ringed tail twitching in brief spasms, amber eyes glazed and fixed as he waited for her to come within reach. And when she did, he was upon her in a flash, his claws like steel daggers as he pinned her to the ground.

A series of sharp cries filled the air.

Then silence.

The slayer of innocents clenched its prey in his jaws and crept into his lair fetid with the stench of decaying flesh. Then, content with his kill, he dropped the limp carcass upon the cold earthen floor and dozed.

A middle-aged woman slid open the glass door that introduced her back porch to the world and stepped out to the wood-planked floor. Her footfalls awoke him immediately, for she tread upon the ceiling of his lair as she gazed upon her great and sprawling garden. It was a virtual wonderland of vibrant flowers and exotic shrubs. She and her husband had worked on the garden for years, and each year it had grown a little more until every inch of her yard was alive with colorful blooms.

As she stood at the edge of her porch, admiring her floral majesty, two hummingbirds appeared. A sudden buzz, then a flash of iridescent green followed quickly by another. They paused in midair to hover on separate sides of her feeder, wings shimmering in the sun as they sampled its sweet nectar. She smiled and watched them drink, delighted by their presence.

Other birds of various breeds and colors flittered among the trees and sang their merry songs. Some sampled the feeders filled with millet and safflower seeds placed around the garden while others tended to the nests they had made in a dozen different birdhouses hanging from trees.

With the pastoral setting the property enjoyed, one would never suspect she lived on a half-acre lot in the center of town, which is precisely why she and her husband had worked so hard to bring a little country to the city. They were ardent nature lovers and birdwatchers, and would often sit on their porch sipping iced tea as they watched the birds, squirrels and rabbits playing about.

But now, as she stood enjoying the cool morning breeze, a waft of unpleasant air came her way. A heavy stench of decay that lingered beneath her nose.

"George!" she cried, opening the glass door into her house. "Come out here right away! Something has died under our porch!"

Her husband carefully folded the newspaper he'd been reading in half and laid it on the table beside him. Then he pushed himself off his favorite overstuffed armchair and shuffled across the living room floor in his slippers and robe.

He stepped out the door and pinched his nose. "Oh my!" he said. "I think you're right."

They descended the seven wooden steps to their lawn together and peered under the porch on their hands and knees. Dead birds and small animals lined the floor in various stages of decomposition. And there was Tiger, crouching among the carnage, wide-eyed and ready to spring.

"Tiger!" the woman shouted. "You bad cat!"

With that, Tiger bolted from under the porch, his orange coat ablaze in the morning sun as he fled through the garden.

"Oh, my goodness," the woman sobbed. "What has Tiger done?"

Her husband put a hand on her trembling shoulder and tried to console her. "He's an outside cat, my dear. All cats are hunters; that's what they do. It's…its natural."

"But there must be something we can do to stop him," she said through her tears. "This is terrible!"

"I can take him to my brother's place. He has ten acres in the country. Lots of room for Tiger to roam. I'm sure he'd be happy there."

"But I *love* Tiger," his wife sobbed. "I couldn't bear to lose him."

Her husband took a hanky from his back pocket and handed it to her. "Tell you what," he said. "I'll enclose the bottom of the porch with lattice board. That'll keep Tiger from bringing any more dead animals around."

She patted the tears from her eyes and nodded her head in appreciation. "Today?" she asked, her tone more a plea than a question.

"Yes," promised her husband. "I'll head over to the lumber store and have the job done before dinner tonight."

Both husband and wife walked quietly into the house, their emotions in disarray. Hers because Tiger was killing so many birds and animals and his because of the extra work (not to mention the expense) that Tiger was about to cause him.

Tiger watched them disappear into the house as he squatted in the children's sandbox next door. Then he cuffed a spatter of sand over the mess he'd just made and hurried back toward the porch he had fled moments ago. As always, there would be a fresh bowl of cat food awaiting him.

Along the way, he glanced up at a robin's nest snuggled within the protective boughs of a pine. He could hear the cheeping of recent hatchlings.

Good things were yet to come…

It's not that I hate housecats per se; it's just that (with the exception of barn cats for rodent control) I don't think they should be left free to roam outdoors, unrestrained. Since their domestication in the Middle East ten thousand years ago, the population has grown to five hundred million cats worldwide. They are the primary cause of death for birds and animals in the United States and have a greater negative impact on wildlife species than habitat destruction, pesticides and death by motor vehicles combined. A recent study by the Smithsonian Institute and the US Fish & Wildlife Service shows that feral and domestic cats kill more than two billion birds and twelve billion mammals each year. To put that number in perspective, a billion minutes ago, Jesus was alive. A billion hours ago, our ancestors were living in the Stone Age.

Many folks don't think their beloved and well-fed kitty is a killer. But there have been many studies on free roaming cats that prove differently.

Research from the University of Georgia, where sixty domestic housecats were fitted with cameras, found that almost half were aggressive hunters. It also showed them eating roadkills, dodging automobiles, drinking sewer water, and interacting with strange cats, increasing their risk for rabies, distemper, and other diseases like toxoplasmosis, which poses significant risks to pregnant women and people with immune deficiencies.

A study from the University of Nebraska states that cats have been responsible for the extinction of thirty-three bird species worldwide. Studies also show that only twenty-five percent of the wildlife killed by cats are brought home. Considering that only a quarter of the actual kills are counted in these studies, the total number must be staggering.

Researchers at the University of Wisconsin estimate that cats in that state kill hundreds of millions of creatures a year, and that they kill forty-seven million rabbits in the U.S. annually.

A biologist at the University of Massachusetts claims hunting behavior is innate in kittens and taught to them by their parents. His studies show that cats continue to hunt even when not hungry. "Domestic cats do not hunt of necessity," he explains. "They hunt for pleasure."

People say that man is the only animal that hunts for sport. That is simply not true, as illustrated in the preceding paragraphs. And unlike housecats, most hunters make use of the animals they kill. The meat is eaten, feathers can be used for fishing lures, and the skins of some critters can be sold into the fur and leather trade. Additionally, hunters are guided by seasons and bag limits. Cats are not. They kill when wildlife mothers are nursing their young, slaughtering nestlings and newborns with unbridled relish.

When a cat steps outside, it begins hunting almost immediately and will kill anything it can catch for the sheer pleasure of tearing it to pieces. The studies above show that housecats pose a worldwide threat to wildlife, especially birds and mammals. Unfortunately, many people refuse to accept the facts about free roaming cats.

In 1966 the U.S. cat population was estimated at thirty million. By 1987 it soared to sixty million and presently stands at more than seventy million housecats.

It is my personal opinion that housecats may be responsible for a drastic decline in several Pennsylvania mammals, such as cottontail rabbits, the least weasel, and the least shrew, which is an endangered species.

Many humane shelters advocate the spaying and neutering of housecats, which would go a long way toward controlling the huge number of free-roaming cats nationwide. But if that's not an option, consider adding a bell to your cat's collar; it just might give some of our precious wildlife an opportunity to escape.

Published June, 1996

There is always one moment in childhood when the door opens and lets the future in.
~Graham Greene

On Trapping

THE FIRE HALL WAS WALL-TO-WALL trappers with their furs. It had been a good season for most. By the end of the day, we had inspected close to a thousand beaver skins along with hundreds of mink, muskrat, raccoons, fox and coyotes.

The Pennsylvania Trappers Association holds a fur sale in Wyoming County after beaver season ends each year. There are a number of fur buyers present at this annual event, and trappers come from everywhere to haggle over the best price for their hard-earned catch.

I brought two dozen beaver pelts myself. Most of my catch was taken from areas where landowners complained about damage. One particularly large beaver had tipped the scales at fifty-five pounds. Huge for a member of the rodent family, I thought. No wonder they can wreak such havoc. Over the years, I've seen fertile pastures turned into lakes, and public highways rendered impassible due to flooding caused by beaver dams; as a result, I spend a considerable amount of my time, both on and off the job, eradicating these nuisance beavers.

Interestingly, a hundred years ago we had no beavers at all in Pennsylvania. In an effort to reintroduce them, the Game Commission obtained several pairs from Colorado in 1917 and released them in the central part of the state. They were protected until 1934 when a limited trapping season was approved in certain portions of the state. Today, six to ten thousand beavers are trapped annually in Pennsylvania.

In the early eighteen hundreds, beaver hats were extremely popular in Europe, and a single beaver pelt was able to fetch a week's wages. As a result, beavers were hunted and trapped relentlessly throughout America, with wealthy businessmen employing thousands of young men, known as company trappers, to bring in furs from the vast American wilderness.

Another group of men who were free trappers also plied the trade. Numbering only a few hundred in all, many risked their lives in quest of beaver pelts. James B. Trefethen, in his book *An American Crusade for Wildlife* wrote, "In the west, along the Rockies and beyond, the fur trade had molded a new and unique breed of American—the mountain man—perhaps the most colorful to stride the stage of American history.

"In the field, they led lives of almost total freedom, traveling alone or in small groups into every cranny of the West in an endless search for beaver. Each, unless he had an Indian squaw, was his own cook, food gatherer, tailor, physician, blacksmith, gunsmith, and mechanic. Except for occasional contacts with others of his kind or military patrols, his links with civilization for months on end were almost nonexistent."

Because their pelts were so highly valued, the beaver was completely wiped out east of the Rocky Mountains and came close to extermination throughout the rest of America. Fortunately, European hat manufacturers started using nutria fur as a replacement in the mid eighteen hundreds, and as the beaver fur trade began to die, many mountain men became buffalo hunters and scouts for the military and wagon trains heading west.

In fact, had it not been for beaver hats and the subsequent boom of the fur trade, America may not be the powerful nation it is today. The beaver's extraordinary value—as much as one hundred dollars per pelt—started an exploration of our country that likely wouldn't have occurred for decades. No one knew the vast wilderness regions better than the trappers who searched every mountain and valley for beavers and other furs, and the trails they blazed were followed by wagon trains that brought thousands of families across America hoping to find a better way of life.

And so it was, more than two hundred years after the first trapper set foot in this great nation, that a boy of twelve wearing a white T-shirt, high-top Converse sneakers and faded dungarees sat on the edge of a century-old stone bridge over the Neshaminy Creek hoping to coax a bass to his worm. It was November 1960, the early autumn sun warm on the back of his neck as he watched his red and white bobber float under the bridge and out of sight without so much as a wobble.

He reeled in his line and was about to cast it back upstream when a sharp scream came from a hollow snag on the bank below. Suddenly a muskrat burst from within, followed by a sleek brown mink, its dark fur glistening in the mid-day sun. The mink attacked the muskrat in a blur of wild savagery, its sharp teeth at the back of its neck, tearing into muscle and flesh. It was over in a matter of seconds, and the boy watched in awe as the mink dragged its prey back into the hollow snag.

That boy was my brother, John. Astonished by what he had witnessed, he couldn't wait to tell me about it. And when I met him later in the day, fishing rod and bait can in hand, he suggested that we start a trapline. "Furs are worth a lot of money," he assured me. "We could make a fortune!"

We both loved the outdoors, and the prospect of earning money from a trapline was exciting to say the least, so we decided to purchase some traps right away. We couldn't afford to buy new, so we began asking friends at school if they knew anyone who had used traps for sale. It didn't take long before we learned of a classmate named Lance who wanted to sell some traps that his father had owned for twenty-five cents apiece. We purchased a dozen and set them along the creek, expecting to catch some muskrats the following morning. But to our dismay, the traps remained empty for days on end, their steel jaws gaping at us in mute testimony.

Hoping Lance would know how to get the muskrats to step into our traps, I sat across from him during lunch at the school cafeteria and waited patiently as the stocky farm boy wolfed down a huge plate of raviolis, mashed potatoes, green beans, and peach slices (all for only thirty-five cents). As soon as he finished eating, I asked him how in the world his father managed to catch muskrats in the traps he'd sold us.

Lance took a big gulp from his milk carton, wiped his mouth with the back of his hand, and belched vociferously. "Oh those things," he said with a wrinkled brow. "My dad caught most of his muskrats in Conibears, not jump traps!"

"*Conibears?*" I shot back in bewilderment. "What are they?"

"Killer traps," shrugged Lance. "You stick 'em in front of the den hole, and when the muskrat swims through the trap it kills them instantly."

This sounded like the perfect solution to our problem. I couldn't wait to get my hands on one. "I have a dollar!" I offered, reaching into my pocket to fish it out. "How many will that buy?"

Lance stuck out a meaty hand and I dropped the wrinkled bill into it.

"Tell you what," he said, "take the school bus home with me and I'll give you two Conibears that are like new."

"Deal!" I said eagerly.

Lance looked across the table and eyed the peanut butter and jelly sandwich my mom had packed for me. "Gonna eat that?"

I'd been so focused on talking about trapping that I had forgotten all about it. "Guess not," I said, sliding the sandwich his way. Besides, my appetite had dwindled considerably after watching him practically inhale his own lunch.

While on the school bus with Lance, I hammered him with questions about how to trap. He had very little experience himself, having accompanied his father only on rare occasions while trapping muskrats. But he managed to give me a few good tips on how to use "killer" traps, and he also told me how to make drowning sets when using foothold traps.

When we got off the bus at his farm, he motioned me to follow him into the barn where several dozen rusted traps hung on a wall. Lance pulled two Conibears from the tangled assortment and handed them to me. Then we walked over to an old wooden desk and he opened the top drawer and pulled out a paper catalog. "Take this," he said solemnly. "I want you to have it."

I reached out and took the pamphlet from his hand. It said *O. L. Butcher's Trapping Supplies, Shushan, New York.* "He's a professional trapper," remarked Lance with a reassuring nod. "Before my father died, he talked about him all the time."

"Geez thanks," I said. "This looks really neat!" Then I saw his eyes start to water up and his chin begin to quiver, and I felt terrible. Lance was a big kid, and I knew he didn't want me to see him cry, so I looked down at my Timex wristwatch (Takes a Licking and Keeps on Ticking) and pretended that I had to go.

"Wow! It's late," I exclaimed. "My Mom is gonna kill me!" Then I turned and ran away as fast as my legs could carry me. Looking back, I guess I was running away from myself more than anything. I still had a father, and it frightened me to think about what it would be like if he died as Lance's dad had.

Lance didn't know it, but he changed my life forever that day. On the way home, I began thumbing through the pamphlet and dreamed of becoming a professional trapper like Mr. Butcher. There was a picture of him on the cover: a husky, rugged looking man wearing a checkered shirt and knit cap as he sat on a stump by his log cabin. Dozens of fox and beaver pelts lined the exterior wall behind him, and he became an instant hero to me.

Back home, I showed my brother the catalog and the new traps I had purchased. Excited about the prospect of finding fur in our traps, John began paging through the pamphlet and soon found an advertisement for a book called *The Trappers Guide*, written by Mr. Butcher. "We have to get a copy of this book!" he declared.

"Yeah, that would be cool!" I said. "But I just gave Lance two weeks allowance for two traps. I'm broke!"

"Don't worry, I'll pay for it," said John. "Fair is fair, and since you bought the traps, I'll buy the book." So we borrowed a four-cent stamp from Mom's kitchen drawer (it had a picture of a Pony Express cowboy riding hard), licked it good and stuck it on an envelope containing a dollar bill and a short note to Mr. Butcher asking him about his life as a professional trapper.

Muskrats were the schoolboys' meal ticket back in those days. They were everywhere. Small creeks running through cornfields provided excellent food and cover for them, and local farmers happily granted us permission to trap the voracious furbearers. Some streams were infested with them, and damage to the banks caused by their constant tunneling was dramatic. Nevertheless, my brother and I had but a handful of traps and were only allowed to set them on weekends while school was open. As a result, we did little to help control the burgeoning muskrat populations.

But things began to change when we received O. L. Butcher's book. My brother and I were doing homework at the kitchen table when our mother suddenly walked in with a manila envelope in her hand and a smile on her pretty face. "Guess what came in the mail today, boys," she said.

John and I both looked up and grabbed for the package at the same time. "Ah, ah, ah!" Mom cautioned. "Homework comes first."

Needless to say, we finished our homework in record time and soon found ourselves tearing open the package from O. L. Butcher. We were delighted to see that he had sent us a hand-written letter along with his book. I have kept it, along with several others he sent me before he passed away in 1967. In his letter, he wrote:

Dear Bill and John,

I trap for a living and will start after cats and brush wolves for $25 bounty soon after Labor Day. Then will trap mink, muskrats, fisher, coon, and fox as soon as the season opens.

Last spring I trapped 68 beaver and 4 otter — one beaver for each year I am old.

I didn't see that going trapping as a profession was always a poor man's occupation. Only occasionally are furs up to where one makes good wages. But furs will always be in demand as long as pretty girls are—

Thanks, Butch

John and I were thrilled. After all, we were only twelve, and O. L. Butcher *himself* had actually written a letter to us! Gee whiz, he was one of the best trappers in the whole world! His catch of sixty-eight beavers astounded us. And his plans to trap exotic furbearers like brush wolves (eastern coyote) and fishers in the remote Adirondack Mountains of New York had our hearts pounding with unbridled envy.

My brother and I pored through his book, eyes like saucers as we examined the exciting photographs taken from his wilderness traplines. We read every word, studied every set, and memorized every secret the master trapper had revealed. By the time we stopped reading, it was long past our bedtime. But tomorrow was Saturday, and our parents had allowed us to stay up late so we could finish our new book. Excited by all we had learned, we finally turned out the lights and drifted off to sleep, dreaming of meandering streams in faraway places and trapping muskrats by the hundreds.

At precisely six the following morning, my clock radio came alive to the tune of Elvis (The King) Presley singing his latest hit, *It's Now or Never*. John and I leaped out of our beds, slipped into some warm clothes, and tiptoed quietly downstairs so as not to awaken our family. After a quick bowl of Sugar Pops and milk, we grabbed our jackets and rubber boots, and hustled into the garage to get some traps.

As we proceeded toward the creek, armed with our newfound knowledge, I looked at my brother and said, "I think this is the day we become real trappers!"

John offered me a mischievous grin. Then he threw back his head and bellowed, *"IT'S NOW OR NEVVVERRR,"* in a vain attempt to imitate Elvis, causing us both to burst out laughing so hard our bellies started to ache, which made the long walk to Neshaminy Creek go by twice as fast.

It's hard to believe that almost forty years have passed since that day, but I remember it well: The bright, sapphire sky dappled with lazy white clouds; the sun, gentle and warm on our boyish faces; and the earthy scent of autumn leaves as we broke into the woods and raced toward the streambank ahead. But most of all I remember the heart-pounding, heady excitement that two twelve-year-old boys felt each and every day they spent on the trapline.

I will never forget those early days with my brother, John. We shared a sense of adventure few our age could know. Being in the woods and streams, alone, away from human dwellings, scouting for fur, was an indescribable joy. We often imagined ourselves as pioneers—the first to set foot wherever we happened to be!

Trapping transformed our lives in many ways, and we began to mature into men that winter so long ago. Through trapping, we learned about responsibility: when traps are set, they must be checked every day. That was a moral and ethical obligation. Some mornings we would step outside and the cold wind would take our breath away. The temptation to retreat back into the cozy warmth of our home was great, but the allure of the trapline with its curious mysteries and rousing surprises was far greater, and we would stride into the early darkness with our handful of traps in search of adventure.

John and I not only learned about *how* to trap that winter, we also learned a lot about *why*. We discovered that trapping wasn't about making money—it wasn't even about catching fur, really. It was about learning to read sign, like animal tracks and scats; it was about matching wits with animals on their own turf; it was about animal behavior, lures and scents, proper skinning and care of pelts, grading fur; it was about ethics, responsibility, self-respect, purposefulness, and rugged individualism.

Yes, my brother and I got quite an education that first season on the trapline so long ago, and our love for trapping managed to keep us out of trouble while growing up. It also fostered a deep appreciation for our commonwealth's natural resources, which eventually led both of us into careers as state game wardens.

John and I still find time to trap these days, and the trapline continues to teach us things about life. Even now.

Published November 1999

But the wildest of all the wild animals was the Cat.
He walked by himself, and all places were alike to him.
    ~ Rudyard Kipling

The Bobcat at Thurston Hollow

I **WILL NEVER FORGET THE FIRST TIME** I tangled
with a bobcat. These ferocious felines are completely
protected by the state, and they are so rare it's uncommon to
see so much as a single track anywhere. But every once in a
while a trapper will catch one in a trap set for a raccoon or a
fox, prompting a call to the game warden for assistance in
releasing it.

This particular day, I had a cadet from the agency's
Training School with me as I drove out to meet a trapper who
had a bobcat in his trap. The cadet was to be my shadow for
three weeks, and he was thrilled by the prospect of watching
a twenty-year veteran teach him the tricks of the trade.
Because he viewed me as some kind of super woodsman who
knew everything about hunting, trapping, and the outdoors, I
didn't tell him that I'd never released a bobcat from a trap
before. But since I'd been a fur trapper for thirty years myself,
and had considerable experience handling all sorts of critters,
I was sure the bobcat would be no problem for me.

We were in the middle of hunting season and had just
wrapped up an investigation on a deer-baiting incident when
dispatch notified me about the cat. "Head down to Thurston
Hollow," the operator directed. "The trapper will be waiting
along the road for you."

"A bobcat!" said the cadet. "Never saw one before. At least not in the wild, anyway. Just on TV and in the movies."

"They're nocturnal," I said as we wheeled down the state highway toward the hollow. "That's one reason why you don't see them much. This one should weigh between twenty and thirty pounds if it's an adult."

"That's it?" exclaimed the cadet. "I thought they were a lot bigger!"

"They look it," I said. "I picked up a roadkill last month that weighed thirty-five pounds and measured five feet from paw to paw stretched out. That's huge for a bobcat. In the wild, it would have looked twice as big because of its heavy coat. That's why some people mistake them for mountain lions."

The cadet looked at me, his face grim. "Mountain lions?" he said uneasily. "Do you have them here?"

"No. But I've had dozens of supposed sightings over the years. Investigated every one of them, too. They turned out to be everything from housecats to black bears, but no mountain lions."

"Are there a lot of bobcats around?"

"Some states have healthy bobcat populations, but they're rare in Pennsylvania. We only have them in the northcentral and northeastern portions of the state."

"What happened to them?"

"Populations dwindled mostly due to habitat destruction," I said. "Millions of acres were logged off in the early nineteen hundreds. There was also a thirty-five dollar bounty on them for a long time. Thousands were killed until the bounty was discontinued in the late thirties. In 1970 they were put on the protected species list, and they're finally starting to make a comeback now."

"Will the trapper have to pay a fine for catching one?" asked the cadet.

"No," I assured him. "He probably caught it in a fox set. He did the right thing by calling for help. Bobcats can be a real challenge to get out of a trap."

"How are we going to do it?"

"You'll see," I said. "I've done this sort of thing plenty of times before. All you have to do is sit back and watch."

"So I'll get a chance to observe a master at work, huh?"

"Yep," I assured him. "It'll be a good lesson for you, too. Something you can tell the other cadets about when you get back to the Training School in January."

Of course, at the time, I had no idea how much I'd regret saying those words.

When we got to Thurston Hollow, the trapper was standing along the road waiting for us, and I pulled over and rolled down my window. I knew him well. A decent, soft-spoken man who loved the outdoors and spent most every day hunting and trapping during the open season.

"Hi Paul," I said. "Where's the cat?"

"He turned and pointed to a dirt lane that wound its way up the mountain. "It's about a hundred yards up that old logging road. I caught him in one of my fox sets."

"Hop in," I offered. "I'll take you with us."

With that, the cadet opened the passenger door and got out. "Why don't you sit up front, sir," he said. "The back's a mess." Then he shoved some of the clutter out of his way and squeezed into the back.

He was right, the Bronco was a mess. But that's to be expected when you practically live in your patrol vehicle during hunting season. It was basically a rolling workplace equipped citation boxes, clipboards, topographical maps, hunting digests, license revocation lists, pens, papers, extra food, thermos with coffee, sleeping bags, blankets, shotgun, .22 caliber rifle, flashlights, beaver traps and lures, and other assorted odds and ends.

"Thank you, son," said the trapper as he slid in next to me. "You must be new. I haven't seen you around before."

"I'm a cadet from the Game Commission Training School," he said proudly. "I'm assigned to Officer Wasserman for the next three weeks."

"Three weeks! You've got a good teacher, son, but that doesn't seem like enough time for a new game warden to learn everything he'll need to know."

I put the Bronco in gear and headed for the logging trail while the cadet continued talking.

"I've been assigned to four different officers over the next three months before I go back to the school in January," he explained. "I graduate in June of next year. By then I'll have fifty weeks of training under my belt."

The trapper nodded appreciatively. "Well, for now you're with one of the best game wardens around, son. And I've known a few over the past seventy years."

"Yes, sir," said the cadet.

I looked at the trapper. "I'll have that fifty I owe you in the mail next week," I said in an attempt to shake off my blush.

He chuckled softly, then said, "This is the first bobcat I've ever caught. I'd love to keep him, but I know that would be breaking the law. Think we'll ever have a season on them, Bill?"

"I think we will," I said. "Deer hunters are starting to see them in their drives, and trappers are finding them in their traps more frequently. It's just a matter of time."

I popped open the glove box, pulled out a digital camera, and stuffed it into my coat pocket. "I'll get some pictures of the cat and send them to you, Paul. That way you'll have something to remember him by."

"Thanks, Bill," he said. "I'd like that a lot."

The bobcat paid us little attention as I rounded a bend and parked a few yards away. It lay there in the cool grass staring at us curiously. The steel-jawed trap had been set just off the roadway where the trapper had dug a small hole in the ground about two inches wide by six inches deep and baited it with a walnut-sized chunk of muskrat. Foxes and other predators traveled the logging road on a regular basis as they moved from one hunting location to another, but the bobcat had managed to find bait first and had its front paw clasped firmly in the jaws of a number two fox trap.

"He looks so relaxed," said the cadet. "I thought steel traps caused a lot of pain and suffering."

"Not really," I said. "Especially if you use the right sized trap for the animal you're after. They'll fight a trap at first, but after a few minutes they usually quiet down and lie still. I've even come across animals that were sleeping in my traps."

"How are you going to get him out?" asked the cadet.

"I have a snare-pole, but cats tend to strangle easily, so I'd rather not use it at first." I said. "This guy looks so relaxed I might be able to get a blanket over him."

We all piled out of the Bronco and I grabbed a heavy blanket from the back. Bobcats, I knew, were fierce fighters with powerful jaws and sharp claws that can inflict serious damage. My plan was to place the blanket over the bobcat so I could release the trap from its paw without being bitten or scratched. It had worked in the past with other animals, the cover producing a calming effect once the critter couldn't see anything, and I was hoping the bobcat would react the same way.

Holding the blanket like a gallant and gritty matador, I inched toward the cat. But as I attempted to drape it over him, he suddenly came alive, bearing a mouthful of pointy teeth in a clear warning for me to stay back. The trap was anchored to a chain that offered enough room for the cat to take a chunk out of my leg if it wanted, so I quickly backed away feeling somewhat like a fool.

Bobcat bearing his teeth in a warning for me to stay back

It left me with no other option but to use my Ketch-All Pole, a baton style snare-pole with a plastic-coated cable loop that can be tightened around the body or neck of an animal. The pole has a spring-loaded lock-and-release system enabling the animal to be turned loose without contact by the handler. My plan was to snag the cat and release it quickly, before it could injure itself fighting the noose.

I instructed the trapper to stand by until I had the bobcat held securely in my snare-pole. When I gave him a green light, he was to depress the trap springs, freeing its foot, so I could release the noose and set the cat free. All so simple, so I thought.

I extended the telescoping handle as far as it would go, giving me a five foot reach, and then began to slide cautiously toward the bobcat with my noose hanging at the ready. As I moved, I couldn't help envisioning the *Looney Tunes* character Wile E. Coyote tiptoeing toward Roadrunner with a pole-snare of his own. Things always comically backfired for the coyote, and in retrospect, I should have taken my vison as an indication of things to come.

When I was close enough to reach the cat, I slowly lowered my noose, hoping to slip it over his head. But he immediately clamped his jaws on the cable, biting and tearing at it in a wild frenzy. I let him fight the noose until he tired of it and let go, then I quickly slipped it around his neck and cinched it up, causing the bobcat to explode into a boiling rage. But the leverage was all mine, and I quickly pinned the cat to the ground, permitting the trapper to release the trap from its foot.

When I opened the snare, I expected the cat to immediately dash into the surrounding woods. But to my surprise, it dropped on its belly and stared up at me as if daring me to make another move.

"Look at that," said the trapper. "His foot's so numb he thinks he's still in the trap."

I gave the bobcat a poke with my snare-pole to get him moving, but instead of heading for the woods, he ran straight for my patrol car, ducked under the frame, and climbed into the wheel well behind my rear tire.

To make matters worse, a call came over my radio about a poaching incident in progress only a few miles away, so I slid inside the Bronco and grabbed the mic. "Ten-four," I said. "I'm having a problem with my Bronco right now. I'll get there soon as I can."

I needed to get on my way quickly, so I dropped on my belly and began poking at the cat's ribs with my snare-pole hoping to chase him from under my vehicle. Unfortunately, that only encouraged him to crawl deeper into the chassis and climb on top of the gas tank where he wedged himself between it and the undercarriage.

Exasperated, I slid under the Bronco on my back until I came face-to-face with the angry bobcat. Although it was the dead of winter with a frigid wind from the north, I could feel a line of sweat run down the center of my back into the seat of my pants as he peered down at me and hissed menacingly.

"Easy kitty," I breathed, easing my snare loop toward his head. "Daddy's not going to hurt you one little bit."

"You talking to us?" called the trapper.

I turned my head and saw two pairs of boots from under the Bronco's frame. My cadet and the trapper were standing right next to me.

"Just thinking out loud," I said.

"Sounded like you were starting a conversation with that ol' bobcat."

"Very funny," I said in an attempt to hide my embarrassment.

"We thought so too!" snorted the trapper.

Of course, as intended, he managed to get my cadet snickering along with him.

"Okay, you caught me," I admitted with a chuckle of guilt.

"What's going on under there," asked the trapper.

"The bobcat is up on my gas tank," I said. "I think I can reach him with my snare-pole, but I'll need somebody to grab my feet and pull me out."

"I've got you, sir," said the cadet. And I felt his strong hands grab my ankles. "Ready when you are."

"Okay," I said. "I'll let you know when I have him."

I eased my noose up to the cat until it was directly in front of his face. He was boxed in and had no place to go, so I quickly slipped it over his head and drew the cable tight.

"Got him!" I hollered.

The bobcat let out a wild growl, its claws thrashing at the undercarriage for something to cling to, but the Bronco's steel frame offered nothing as the cadet pulled me from under the car with the cat in my snare-pole.

Fearful that it might strangle, I sprinted thirty yards to the wood's edge while the bobcat hung limply in my noose. When I finally released the snare, he dropped to the ground and staggered backwards a few feet, then stood there staring at me.

Anxious to be on my way, I gave him a prod with the snare-pole, and he started padding wobbly-legged into the woods. But to my surprise, he turned suddenly and made a beeline for my Bronco. Fortunately, he was still woozy from the noose, and I managed to sidestep fast enough to block him. He stopped and stared at me drunkenly, and I began to whoop and holler and flail my arms about like a raving lunatic hoping to turn him back (let's face it I was desperate). Thankfully, the bobcat took the hint and scampered back into the woods where he belonged.

I breathed a huge sigh of relief and hurried back to my Bronco hoping I wasn't too late for the poaching incident. I signaled the cadet as I drew near, and he piled in alongside me.

"Gotta go!" I said to the trapper through my open window.

"Thanks for the help," he said. "If I catch another one, I hope it's a lot more sociable."

I smiled in agreement. Then I dropped the Bronco into gear and wheeled down the bumpy logging road toward Tunkhannock.

As I sped down the state highway, I noticed the cadet writing on a notepad from the corner of my eye. "Whatcha writing about?" I asked.

"I just wanted to make sure I remembered all the details when I get back to the Training School."

"Details?"

"Yes, sir. About the bobcat."

I pursed my lips and gave him a stern look. "Did I ever mention that performance evaluation I have to do while you're assigned to me?"

The cadet stiffened in his seat. "N...no, sir," he said, eyeing me cautiously.

"It's a doozey," I said. "My last cadet never made it back to the training school."

"I understand, sir," said the cadet.

I continued down the highway in silence as he tucked his notepad into a coat pocket and stared solemnly out the side window.

"Gotcha!" I said with a mischievous smile.

The cadet whipped his head around and stared at me in open-mouthed surprise. "You sure did," he said with a sigh of relief. Seriously, sir...how am I doing so far?"

"You're doing fine, son," I said. "Now, can I ask *you* a question?"

He regarded me warily for a second. "Of course, sir."

"Can you call me Bill instead of sir all the time? After all, we're partners, you know."

He looked at me for a long moment, his face gleaming with pride. "Yes," he said with a broad smile. "I think I can manage that just fine."

<hr>

Published November 1994

Author's Note

Presently there is a limited open season on bobcats within select wildlife management units in Pennsylvania.

For what we call illusions are often, in truth, a wider vision of past and present realities.
    ~George Elliot

The Passing

NOW THAT SPRING HAS ARRIVED, a number of people have asked about Beauford the cottontail since I wrote about him last winter.

Truth is, I haven't seen Beauford for months. I don't know what happened to him. The snow was piled high when he disappeared, much too deep for him to go anywhere. And he was way too fat to have starved. Besides, there were plenty of firebush plants leftover when he disappeared—even for *his* voracious appetite.

My children often ask about him, too. We used to see him every day. And now it seems he's vanished. My wife and kids really miss that rabbit. I can see it in their eyes.

As for me—nah! I don't miss him at all. There are plenty of rabbits in the world. It's not like they're endangered or anything. Really. Why should I miss him?

My wife thinks I miss him. I tell her I don't but then she says, "How come you keep staring out the kitchen window if you don't miss him?"

I tell her I'm only looking at how green the grass is getting, but she doesn't believe me.

She thinks she knows me…well, actually she knows me pretty well...but I don't miss that rabbit. That would be silly. It's not like he was a dog, for example. Dogs are a man's best friend. No, I don't miss Beauford at all. Although I admit, sometimes I do look for him. But that's only because I don't want that pesky rabbit eating any more of my shrubbery. And if I see him around, I'll be sure to chase him away.

Still, I can't help but wonder what happened to him. Shortly before the snow melted last month, I would see fresh cat tracks on my property every day. No rabbit tracks, just cat tracks. Sometimes I'd even see their footprints in the snow-dust on the hood of my truck. Boy, cats can go anywhere can't they.

Cats are great wanderers, too. I know because they often wander about my property leaving buried treasures for me to find. And are they ever smart! I keep my garbage bags behind my house until trash day, and in practically no time at all my neighbor's cat realized its claws could poke right through the plastic. Boy, are they clever. They use their paws like hands, too, reaching into the hole they've made to pull out all sorts of things. And when a trail of garbage leaks from the torn bags as I carry them to the curb, I just chuckle to myself, walk back, and pick everything up. Then I go inside and scrub my hands clean.

Cats will be cats, I suppose.

Speaking of which, shortly after Beauford disappeared, I dreamed I heard a noise coming from my kitchen, like the scrape of a chair being pulled back. Tiptoeing through the shadows, I went down the hallway and peeked in. There was no need for introductions. It was Beauford, although barely recognizable, his shadowy form outlined against the moonlit room. He was sitting on a kitchen chair wet with blood. One ear was half gone, and his left eye looked like a fried egg.

"Beauford!" I gasped. "What happened to you?" I was so shocked that I could hear the panic in my own voice (can you do that in dreams?).

Oh, you noticed, huh. Thought you might.

"Noticed! Good grief!"

What do you think happened, Bill? I'll give you three guesses.

"C'mon, Beauford, just tell me. Man, you look bad!"

Look who's talking. Did you ever peek into a mirror after you just woke up? Not a pretty sight, big guy.

"Very funny," I said. "Now tell me what happened to you."

Cat got me. You know, people ought to keep them inside, they're so...uncivilized. But really, I didn't come here to complain.

"What cat? Whose cat?" I roared.

Hey, quiet down. You'll wake the whole family. It was white. White as snow. That's all I can tell you.

"I never saw one like that around here," I said.

Wish I could say the same.

Beauford looked down for a moment, and I watched a pearl of blood roll along the bridge of his nose and fall to the floor.

Tell the kids I was asking for them, okay? he said.

I nodded stiffly. Then I watched in silenced awe as he slowly disappeared, his shadowy form transmuting into the vague outline of a human before fading into the darkness like...well, like a ghost.

And though he was gone, I could feel a presence in the room. And suddenly an embrace—the strength of it astonishing. I felt a thickly muscled chest...and the fading beat of a heart. Then something wet and warm soaking into my shirt.

Blood, I thought grimly. It must be blood...

"Bill! Are you all right?" It was my wife, her voice groggy with sleep."

I bolted awake with a vice-like pressure on my chest. My nightshirt, drenched with sweat, clung to my flesh like a wet rag. I threw my covers off and sat on the edge of the bed, the alarm clock telling me it was three o'clock in the morning.

"I'm fine," I said. "Bad dream. That's all."

Wide awake, I went to a drawer and put on a dry nightshirt. Then I walked down the darkened hallway into the kitchen and was immediately drawn to the window. A huge silver moon cast a dull glow over the landscape, and I could see the outline of the trees dotting my property, their naked branches like long boney arms. As I gazed outside, mesmerized by the tranquil beauty of the early morning hour, my throat suddenly thickened. Just below my window, a housecat materialized from within the shadows. It was white. White as snow. And I watched in dazed astonishment as it slithered across my lawn and disappeared into the night.

Published April 1993

Children have never been very good at listening to their elders, but they have never failed to imitate them. They must, they have no other models.
~James Baldwin

Tommy and his Dad

THEY DID EVERYTHING TOGETHER. When Little League season came around, you could see them playing catch on the front lawn. Tommy was a pitcher, and he could throw a mean fastball thanks to his father's constant encouragement. His dad would practice with him every afternoon, squatting in a catcher's stance taking pitch after pitch until his knees ached so bad he would have to call it a day. He went to all of Tommy's games, sharing in his joy when the team would win and in his sorrow whenever a loss would come.

In between baseball games and practice sessions, Tommy and his dad would often take long walks together hunting arrowheads in the surrounding fields. Sometimes they'd get lucky and stumble upon a big find—like the summer they discovered a stone spearhead poking out of a plow furrow on John Pittner's farm. Elated over their find, they danced like fools in the hot summer sun until they fell to the ground exhausted.

Later that day, they sat in the shade and shared a picnic lunch: baloney and square cheese slapped between two slices of white bread and trimmed with yellow mustard. Tommy's favorite. While munching on sandwiches, they talked about the big game coming up later that evening. The Phillies were playing against the New York Mets, and Tug McGraw would be facing sluggers like Darryl Strawberry and Mike Piazza. But with Pete Rose catching and Mike Schmidt on third, the Phillies would be tough to beat. They planned on watching the game on TV over a giant bowl of popcorn and could hardly wait until it started.

Along with Little League games and arrowhead hunting, Tommy and his dad also enjoyed bicycling and hiking together. But there were two things his father never included Tommy in: hunting and trout fishing. They had gone for sunfish and bluegills plenty of times but never trout. And whenever Tommy asked to go with him, his father would tell him to wait until he was a little older because he wasn't ready to learn the ropes yet.

When Tommy turned ten, his father gave him a brand new fishing rod for his birthday to replace the cheap plastic one he'd been using for panfish. It had an open-faced Mitchell reel, just like his dad's. Tommy couldn't believe his eyes. "Thanks, Dad!" he said excitedly. "Does this mean you're gonna take me trout fishing now?"

His dad surprised him when he smiled and said, "Yup! Season opens tomorrow. Are you ready?"

More than anything, Tommy wanted to know the secrets of catching trout. To learn the ropes, as his father would say. He ran to his father and hugged him tight. "This is the best birthday present in the whole world! Thanks, Dad!"

"You'll have to go to bed early tonight," said his father. "We're heading out before dawn."

When Tommy's alarm rang at four o'clock the next morning, he ran down the hall into his bedroom to shut it off. Too excited to sleep, he'd been in the living room watching cartoons on TV.

Tommy's dad walked into his bedroom wearing slippers and a robe. "Up before your old man, huh?"

"Yes, Dad, and I'm ready to go. I couldn't sleep."

His father nodded understandingly. "First rule for all fishermen: Have a good breakfast and you'll have a good day! Pancakes and sausage sound good to you?"

Tommy's stomach growled at the mere mention of food. "Sounds real good!"

"Okay, here's the plan: You get the kitchen ready, and as soon as I'm shaved and dressed, I'll rustle up some food for the two of us. Deal?"

"Deal!"

After breakfast, they piled into the family car and drove to a stream that had recently been stocked with trout. As they walked along the bank, Tommy was amazed to see anglers lining the shore almost shoulder to shoulder. There were so many fishing lines in the water he wondered how they kept them all from tangling. It didn't take long before he realized they didn't when someone yelled angrily at the man next to him as he reeled in a trout that had twisted in his line.

Some anglers wore hip boots and stood in the stream's center, casting to the opposite shore before reeling in their lures. Tommy noticed that they seemed to have better control of their equipment and managed to stay clear of the others fishing along the banks.

"Look at those fools," his dad remarked. "Too lazy to walk." He pointed toward a cove in the distance. "That's where they'll be, Tommy. And they'll be hitting hard when we get there."

Dawn was breaking as they approached the cove. Long fingers of sunlight filtered through the trees, melting the smoky haze that hung over the languid waters ahead. A great blue heron lifted off shore, its six-foot wingspan pushing lazily through the fog in long and graceful sweeps. Tommy stopped to stare at the giant bird as it faded into the gray mist. He'd never seen one before, and felt as if he'd been transported back in time when prehistoric monsters roamed the earth, for the great bird looked like one of the gigantic winged pterodactyls he'd learned about in science class.

"Tommy! You coming?" called his dad.

Tommy snapped out of his trance and ran to catch up. "Yes, sir," he called. "Coming right now."

As father and son fished the icy stream, Tommy began to wonder when he was going to learn the ropes. So far, the day was no different from when they'd gone after sunfish and bluegills, except that trout fought much harder than the panfish he was used to. His first brookie startled him when it leaped wildly from the water as he reeled it close to the bank, and he left the line slack just long enough for it to escape. Tommy's dad chuckled as his son stared in wonder at his empty hook.

"Don't worry, Tommy," said his father. "There's plenty more of 'em. Next time wait till they pull hard on the bait before you set your hook. Trout can be real slippery."

Tommy took his dad's advice and soon landed his next fish. He dropped the brookie into his creel and marveled at how its coloring changed from olive-green along its upper back to a marbled yellow pattern on its sides with a bright orange belly. "Wow, Dad!" he cried. "They sure are pretty."

His dad smiled contentedly. "Good eating, too. Keep after 'em, Tommy."

Before long, Tommy had three trout in his creel. He knew his dad had caught more fish than he did, and was about to ask how many when he saw a man dressed in green walking along the bank fifty yards away.

"Who's that guy, Dad?" he asked innocently.

Tommy's dad turned and saw the man working his way toward them. "That's the game warden Tommy," he said in a low voice. "Come over here and take two of my trout."

"But why, Dad?"

"'Cause I said so, Tommy. Now hurry up!"

Tommy started toward his dad when the warden stopped abruptly and pulled a hand-held radio from his belt. He spoke into it briefly, then did a quick one-eighty and started back downstream toward the road.

"Whew!" his dad breathed. "Close one, Tommy. He must be after somebody."

Tommy was bewildered by his father's behavior and couldn't understand why he was acting so strangely.

"What's a game warden, Dad?" he asked.

"He's the guy who goes around harassing people like us, checking licenses, bag limits—stuff like that."

"What's a bag limit?"

"It's what those dummies who write game and fish laws say you're allowed keep. If you're hunting rabbits, it's four per day. If you're trout fishing, it's five."

Tommy looked at his dad questioningly. "Is that why you wanted me to take two of your fish?"

His dad eyed him sternly. "I know what you're thinking, Tommy, so let me explain. We don't get a chance to go fishing very often, do we?"

Tommy nodded.

"Well, it works like this: Some guys are out here fishing every day of the week, but we only go fishing on Saturdays, right?"

"Yes, sir."

"Well then, what difference does it make if I catch fifteen trout in one day and the guy down the street catches fifteen trout in seven days? We both end up with the same number of trout for the week, right?"

Tommy shrugged. "I guess so."

"Well I *know* so. It's only fair. Now let's get our lines back in the water and see who can catch the biggest fish."

And so, as Tommy grew older, his dad would take him hunting and fishing with him every chance he got. And Tommy was taught to poach wildlife and evade the game warden at every turn.

Years later, while sitting in math class staring at Mr. Bopinski's back as he drew complicated formulas on the board, Tommy wondered how he would ever manage to pass the upcoming exam. He was the quarterback for his high school football team, and they had a new coach this year who drilled them into the ground at daily practice sessions. On top of that, there was a brand new playbook to deal with. Tommy would come home exhausted every day. Too tired to study, his grades were slipping, especially in math class.

"*Psst!* Hey, Tommy!"

Tommy snapped out of his daze and looked to his right. Bo Johnson, a teammate and close friend, sat across from him with a hand cupping his mouth. "I've got a cheat sheet," he whispered. "See ya at lunch."

Tommy whipped his head back at the teacher. He was still drawing diagrams on the board. As far as Tommy was concerned, he might as well be writing Chinese symbols because none of it made any sense to him. He was doomed to failure. And if he didn't pass the test, the coach would throw him off the team. That was a rule every player was subjected to. The biggest game of the year was coming up: Bulldogs vs. Warriors. And without Tommy as quarterback, they'd be crushed. He looked at Bo and nodded. Then he turned back and stared at the drawings on the board, his eyes glazing over with boredom.

F ive anxious teammates huddled around a lunch table and stared in awe as Bo Johnson wolfed down the third plate of spaghetti that had been slid his way.

"How can you eat that stuff?" said Tommy. "It tastes like slimy boogers!"

Bo wiped his mouth with the back of his hand and smiled. His teeth stained red from spaghetti sauce. "You might think that's funny but it's snot."

With that, the whole table broke into uproarious laughter. Bo had a unique way of relieving tension when things got tense, like right now when everybody was stressed out about a math final. He always managed to come up with a silly one-liner that would crack them up. Sometimes it wasn't the joke so much as his dopey smile and the way he'd roll his eyes when he said it. Everybody liked Bo Johnson, including his teachers. He was the class clown, an outstanding athlete, and to the envy of many of his friends, extremely popular with the girls. But one thing Bo Johnson didn't have was integrity. And although he was good at cracking jokes, he wasn't much for cracking the books, and managed to get through many of his classes by cheating on tests.

Tommy leaned toward Bo. "What about the test?" he said in a low voice. "You said you have something?"

Bo shifted his eyes left and right, then grinned slyly at his teammates. They leaned forward simultaneously. All eyes were on him. He took a quick glance around the lunchroom to make sure they weren't being spied on. The kids at the surrounding tables were absorbed in their own affairs, eating and talking and joking with each other. "I got the answers to every question on the test," he said confidently. "You guys don't have a thing to worry about." He dug into the front pocket of his jeans and pulled out a wad of notebook papers folded into tiny squares. Pinching them between his thumb and forefinger, he flicked them one-by-one around the table as if dealing a deck of cards.

"I made one for each of you," he said. "But don't open them now, somebody might see you."

Tommy stared at him in wonder. "How in the world did you get this?"

Bo looked back at him with a smug grin. "Guess who's dating Bopinski's daughter."

"And she went along with this!" said Tommy, incredulous.

"Well, not at first—she's a good kid. But as you know, she's also one of our cheerleaders. So when I told her half the team was gonna flunk the test unless I got the answers, she offered to help."

"I wish you wouldn't have done that," said Tommy.

Bo cocked his chin and eyed him sternly. "Done what? Save your sorry butt?"

"I just don't think you should've gotten her involved."

"You like her, don't you!" Bo replied in surprise. "I can see it in your eyes."

"Apparently more than you do!" said Tommy.

Bo shrugged off the comment. "Chalk it up to team spirit," he said coolly. "She wants to help. Besides, it's game over without the answers and you know it."

Tommy stared back at Bo for a long moment. "You got spaghetti sauce on your shirt, doofus," he said.

T ommy sat at his desk with his left arm folded across the top of his test paper as Mr. Bopinski sifted through a stack of exams from the last class. Bopinski had his red pen out and was doing a lot of marking. Not a good sign. The kids called him The Big Bopper behind his back. Nobody would dare say it to his face. Mr. Bopinski was a big man with a violent temper. Tommy had walked into his class once and found blood drops on the floor. Rumor had it Bopinski threw a disorderly student into the wall and busted open his nose. Everybody was scared of him (except Bo Johnson who was crazy enough to date Bopinski's daughter behind his back), even the other teachers.

Every once in a while, Bopinski would stick his head up and look over the classroom. Tommy had to be real careful not to get caught. To that end, he'd written the answers on his arm, just above his wrist, so his shirtsleeve would hide them. They were penned in ink. Four neat horizontal lines that took up a single square-inch of flesh.

The test had twenty questions that could be answered in alphabetical choice: *a*, *b*, *c*, or *d*. Tommy waited until Bopinski had a particularly bad test, one that required a lot of red marks, before slipping a pinky finger under his cuff to see the answers. He was in no hurry. He didn't want to finish before everybody else; it might raise suspicion with his teacher, who was well aware that he was struggling in his class. He glanced over at Bo Johnson and the five other teammates in the room. They were playing it cool, too.

When the buzzer finally went off, signaling the end of class, Tommy stood up and laid his test on Mr. Bopinski's desk along with the other kids as they filed out of the room.

But as he stepped into the long hallway jammed with students heading for their next class, he felt a heavy hand on his shoulder and turned around. Tommy almost fainted when he looked into the steely eyes of The Bopper.

"I just took a look at your test," he said.

Tommy couldn't breathe; certain he'd been caught, his heart pounded wildly.

Instead, his teacher smiled and said, "Looks like you did pretty well. Congratulations! Wish I could say the same for some of my other students."

Tommy tried to speak but his throat was cement. He forced a weak smile, blinking stupidly at his teacher.

Bopinski launched a fist into the air (Tommy flinched). "Go Warriors!" he cried, beaming with pride. "See you at the game." Then he turned and walked back into the classroom.

Tommy felt his stomach flip. His breakfast cereal was working its way north fast. He raced down the hallway, squeezing frantically between students as he made a mad dash for the Boys Room. He flung open the door, relieved not to see a pair of feet under the stall ahead. Then he ran to the toilet, dropped to his knees, and puked.

The following morning, Tommy sat at his desk and watched the expressions on his fellow students as Bopinski handed back their tests one by one. He took his time about it, too. Tommy figured it was to make them all suffer. And with the exception of a few eggheads, most of the students looked pretty miserable when they saw their papers.

Bopinski held on to the tests for Tommy and his teammates until all the others had been passed out. Then he announced their names and politely asked them to stand. Tommy figured he was going to congratulate them in front of the class for their perfect scores, but he was dead wrong.

"Report to the principal's office immediately!" Bopinski instructed them. "This institution takes a very dim view on cheating."

Tommy and his teammates filed out of the room like a line of convicts heading for the gallows. They made their way down a long, empty hallway listening to the faded voices of teachers instructing their students as they walked past their classrooms. They could see the kids sitting at their desks through the windowed doorways, some with raised hands and eager faces, hoping the teacher would call on them for the answer. Tommy shook his head, wishing he were one of them, safe inside his classroom. Instead, he'd been singled out by his teacher and castigated as a liar and a cheat. It was the lowest period of his young life and he hated it.

The main office was at the end of the hallway and hemmed with glass windows, which meant every student walking by would be able to see them, adding to their embarrassment. Tommy opened the door and held it for his teammates (not to be polite, but to delay his own entrance for a few precious seconds) allowing them to file into the room. Three secretaries were busily sorting through papers and answering phone calls as they walked in. One of them, the only pretty one, looked up and smiled politely. "Mr. Fishburn is expecting you boys," she said. Then she pointed a slim finger to an open door at the back of the room. "Go right into his office."

Mr. Fishburn eyed them sourly as they walked in. He sat at a desk piled high with manila folders and assorted papers, the wall behind him lined with framed degrees and family photographs. He was short and plump, a thick mass of snow-white hair covering his peculiarly large head. He wore a white shirt with black suspenders and a red bow tie, his trademark uniform that he sported every day.

He leaned back in his chair and laced his stubby fingers behind his head, eyes cold and gray. "Know how you got caught?" he said with a self-congratulatory smile.

Nobody dared answer. Instead, they stood fencepost straight, waiting for him to tell them anyway.

"One of you, and I don't know which—nor do I care," he paused and looked them over one by one, "got a little sloppy. Whoever got the answers to the test and passed them along, managed to reverse the letter *b* with the letter *d* on one of the answers. As a result, not only did you all get nineteen out of twenty questions right—which is completely out of character for each of you—but you all got the same answer wrong as well." He rocked forward and smacked both hands on his desk in a gesture of finality. "Your three-day suspension begins tomorrow. Additionally, you'll receive an F in math for the year, which means you'll have to make it up in summer school. And no football...but you already know that, don't you." He leaned back in his chair and waved his hand dismissively. "Now get out of here and go back to your class."

Tommy broke the news to his dad later that evening after he finished stacking the dinner dishes. His father listened in silence, his expression slowly changing from shock and bewilderment to a look of pained disappointment...then anger.

"There are rules of conduct when you're in school, Tommy, and you know it!" his dad scolded. "Cheating on tests is an obvious violation of those rules. I can't believe you could do something like that!"

Tommy bowed his head and sighed audibly. "I'm sorry, Dad."

"Sorry for what?" his dad said bitterly. "Getting caught!"

"No. I'm sorry you don't understand."

His father stared back at him, astonished by his response. "What are you talking about, son?

Tommy saw the incomprehension in his father's face and his eyes welled with tears.

"Dad," he sobbed, "why do you get to break the rules of conduct when you're hunting and fishing, but tell me I can't do the same when I'm in school? Don't you see? I'm no different than you, Dad. Your son is just like you."

Published November 1995

109

Bandit

THE THREE CUBS WERE BORN on a chilly April morning in the cavity of a great oak tree. They weighed a mere three ounces at birth, and were covered in yellow-gray fur with a faint black mask and lightly banded tails. Incapable of opening their eyes, the tiny cubs were totally dependent on their mother and spent their early days nursing under the comfort of her warm belly.

But that was five long weeks ago. Now, with their ears alert and eyes wide open, a whole new world awaited them. The largest and strongest cub, a male, was first to clamber up the rough inner wall of the hollow tree that had sheltered them since birth. Reaching the top, he poked his head out the opening, looked down at the vast sea of grass below, and climbed out. His mother lay flattened on a stout branch above. Asleep in the warm afternoon sun, she was unaware her cub was performing a dangerous balancing act on the limb just below.

He managed to hold on for several seconds before losing his balance and plummeting toward the ground. Fortunately, a willowy branch several feet below broke his fall, and another after that, until at last he hit the ground with a soft bounce and lay in the grass on his belly.

Frightened and alone, he let out a high-pitched chattering cry for his mother. She awakened instantly and ran along the limb she'd been sleeping on until she reached the oak's trunk, then she shimmied down tail first, looking over her shoulder and calling to her cub in a burst of raspy barks as she went.

Halfway to her cub, she saw the black Lab. It came straight for him, a low growl in the back of its throat. And had it not been for the heavy leash anchored to the Lab's doghouse, he would have reached him. Instead, the Lab stood straining at the end of his chain, choking in its suffocating grip, mere yards from the helpless raccoon.

In a desperate attempt to rescue her cub, his mother clung to the tree and called to him in a series of soft mews. But he had neither the strength nor the will to attempt another climb, and curled into a ball, trembling with fear.

Young Jacob had just walked into the kitchen to get some milk from the fridge when he glanced out the window and saw his Labrador retriever straining so hard at the end of his leash that his front legs were off the ground. Something was out there, and Duke was going crazy trying to get at it.

Jacob dashed out the back door and ran to his dog's side. "What's the matter boy?" he said. "What do you see?"

The muscular Lab glanced up at him, then back at the tree, a long string of saliva hanging from his mouth as he moaned in excitement. Jacob didn't see anything at first, and patted Duke's head in an attempt to calm him down, "It's all right boy," he said, scanning the surrounding woods. "There's nothing out there."

But the Lab knew better and started barking frantically, which sent the mother raccoon scurrying into her den twenty feet above.

Jacob caught her from the corner of his eye and stared in awe as she disappeared into the tree. "A raccoon!" he said in surprise. "Looks like you were right, Duke."

But the Lab continued to pull at his chain, his black coat shivering with excitement.

"What is it boy?" said Jacob. "See something else?"

Yes! There it was! Curled in the grass by the tree. A baby raccoon! Jacob ran over and plucked the cub from the ground. It thrashed and squirmed in his grip, expelling a desperate series of birdlike cries. In an effort to calm it down, Jacob pulled the front of his T-shirt out of his pants, wrapped the cub inside and pressed it against his belly. Concealed in the cloth cocoon, the frightened cub soon became quiet and snuggled against the comfort of Jacob's warm body.

Jacob turned and started back toward his house just as his mother stepped outside to see what all the commotion was about.

"Mom!" he cried, when he saw her. "Come quick!"

His excitement was so high that his shouts of joy sounded more like panicked cries of pain, sending a jolt of terror into his mother's heart. And when she noticed his T-shirt wrapped in a ball and pushed tight against his stomach, she was certain he'd injured himself.

"Jacob, what's wrong?" she cried, rushing toward him. "Are you hurt?"

Jacob ran to her and shook his head. "No, Mommy, he gasped. "I'm fine. But look what I found!" He opened his T-shirt for a peek at the cub, then quickly closed it again.

"You scared me half to death young man!" his mother said, clutching her chest. "All this commotion over a raccoon!"

"Can we keep him Mom? Can we?"

"Now, Jacob," she cautioned, "you know I don't have time to fool with baby animals, they need too much care."

"You won't have to, Mom. I'll feed him, play with him, clean up after him and everything. I promise!"

"That's what you said about Duke," his mother reminded him. "But who looks after him now?"

"That was a long time ago. I was only ten then, but I'm eleven now! I can do it Mom. I *know* I can."

Jacob's mother had her doubts, but her heart began to melt as she looked into his pleading eyes, and she couldn't help but give in. "Okay, Jacob," she said hesitantly. "We'll give it a try. But if you neglect that animal…"

"I won't Mom. I promise!"

"We'll see about that," she said. "Now, let's get some warm milk into his tummy and find something to keep him in."

Jacob's mother had to admit he was a cute little fella; she actually enjoyed looking after him occasionally. And it was she who named him Bandit because of his black mask. He was surprisingly vocal for his young age, and would growl and hiss and twitter like a bird almost constantly. She taught Jacob how to feed the cub by taking a clean syringe from a medicine bottle and filling it with kitten formula purchased at the local Walmart. Bandit didn't know what to do with it at first. After all, he was used to his mother's nipple. But he soon grew accustomed to the plastic syringe and would lick the formula off the tip. Within a week, he graduated to a baby bottle and would lay on his stomach and suck vigorously on the rubber nipple until his belly was full.

As soon as Bandit was weaned, Jacob started feeding him puppy chow along with some occasional fruits. He especially loved bananas but enjoyed apples, grapes and just about anything sweet. Bandit grew fast, and when he was three months old, he started eating regular dog food and leftover table scraps. Jacob taught him to use a litter box, too, and provided him with his own separate box far away from his mother's cat so they wouldn't tangle.

One day Jacob filled the bathtub with an inch of water and dumped in a dozen minnows and some crawfish he'd caught in the creek near his house. He put Bandit in the tub and watched as the young raccoon stared straight ahead while feeling around in the water with his front feet until he caught a crawfish. But when he picked it up, the crawfish pinched him with both claws. Bandit snorted in surprise and quickly chewed it up. After that, he was careful to pick all the crawfish up just behind their claws so they couldn't pinch him.

The minnows were another matter altogether. They were too fast for Bandit to catch by feel, so he learned to be still until one came within reach, then he'd pounce on it like a cat and trap it in both front paws.

Bandit stayed in a wire dog crate inside the house when Jacob was in school. But every afternoon, when he came home, he'd take Bandit out and let him have the run of the house. The raccoon was extremely curious and bright and loved to play. One of his favorite toys was an old rubber ball that Duke had played with when he was a puppy. Jacob would roll it across the hardwood floor and watch Bandit scamper after it. After pouncing on the ball, Bandit would flop on his back and twirl it around on his chest, waiting for Jacob to come over and snatch it away so he could chase it again.

In those days, they were inseparable. Jacob loved spending time with Bandit, and he kept his promise to his mother by taking full responsibility for his new pet.

Twelve months later, things had changed considerably for the raccoon. Bandit had his own doghouse out back, strategically placed a reasonable distance from Duke's. The big Lab didn't care much for Bandit (an appropriate name for the mischievous raccoon, who'd become unmanageable in recent months, destroying anything he didn't consider food), who now remained tied to a four-foot chain.

A week after being "rescued" by Jacob, Bandit's two sisters had wandered within reach of Duke's chain. He promptly ate them both, making Bandit the sole survivor of his mother's litter. But survival as a shackled captive wasn't much of a life. Pacing for hours at the end of his chain each day, he had become a surly prisoner.

Jacob rarely had time for him now, and on most days he didn't do much more than give the lonely raccoon some food and water. Bandit just wasn't the same anymore and couldn't be trusted, especially since he'd bitten Jacob. It happened when he was walking through the house shirtless with Bandit on his shoulder and accidentally stepped on his toy ball. Jacob lost his balance and pitched forward, causing Bandit to dig his claws into his skin for support. And when Jacob grabbed Bandit by a leg to pull him off, the startled raccoon bit him on the ear.

Jacob put a hand to his head and howled in pain, prompting Bandit to jump to the floor and hide under the couch. Blood was streaming down the side of Jacob's face when his mother rushed into the room. She turned white when she saw him. "My Lord!" she wailed. "What happened to you?"

His mother wanted to get rid of the raccoon after that, but Jacob had begged her to let him keep Bandit. It took a lot of pleading but she finally consented as long as the raccoon stayed outside.

Jacob was a little afraid of Bandit since that day and was reluctant even to bring food out to him, but his mother insisted. After all, her son had pleaded with her to keep the raccoon, and it remained his obligation to feed him. The fact that it had become untrustworthy and aggressive was a good lesson in life for young Jacob, she reasoned. Things don't always turn out the way you think they will. You take the bad with the good and deal with it. That's how you grow as a human being. That's how you become strong and self-reliant. She expected Jacob would eventually set the raccoon free;

after all, it was no good as a pet any longer. But it was a decision she wanted him to make on his own.

Weeks later, while delivering Bandit's food one day, Jacob thought about letting him go. Setting a bowl of dogfood mixed with table scraps down in front of him, he watched as Bandit polished off the meal, and wondered if he could survive in the wild after being raised in captivity. The thought was a sobering one. Even though they'd grown apart, he couldn't bear the notion of Bandit lying in the woods alone somewhere, dying from starvation.

Jacob reached out cautiously and began to stroke Bandit's head. Then he slowly put his hands under his front legs and lifted him off the ground. He talked to him in soft, affectionate tones, telling him he was a good boy and how they might be friends again. Friends forever.

Jacob's Lab watched them from inside his doghouse, growing more jealous by the second until he finally bolted to the end of his chain and barked savagely at them.

Bandit immediately panicked and nipped Jacob on the back of his hand, drawing blood once again.

Jacob dropped the raccoon and kicked him back. "Get away!" he screamed. "Get away!" And Bandit, frightened and confused, ran into his doghouse to hide.

When I got the call about a raccoon bite, I responded immediately. Raccoons are especially susceptible to rabies because they're social animals that often congregate with other raccoons in their area. Along with skunks, they are among the most commonly listed carriers of the dread disease in North America. Rabies is always fatal (only one known case of survival in the world) unless treated before incubation. The virus is spread among mammals via their saliva, typically through a bite, where it travels up the nervous system to the brain, which generally takes about a week. The symptoms don't appear until a few days before death. By then it's too late for a cure, so a potential victim must receive medical care as soon as possible. Treatment is conducted through a series of intramuscular injections with vaccines containing antibodies. If immunized in time, the vaccination is highly effective and the patient's recovery is almost certain.

I explained all this to Jacob and his mother as we stood in their kitchen together. I told them that I was especially concerned because the raccoon had been kept outside for the past several months and could have been exposed to the disease. Although the Lab had been vaccinated for rabies, the raccoon had not, and needed to be tested immediately.

"You mean you're gonna take Bandit away?" asked Jacob, his face a mask of concern.

His right hand had a white bandage on it. I could see a small circle of blood in its center. "The raccoon broke skin," I said. "He has to be tested for rabies."

"Well, good riddance to him!" said his mother. "Should've told Jacob to release the thing a long time ago, but I wanted him to make up his own mind about it." She put an arm around her son and pulled him tight. "Now he's been bitten, and it's all my fault."

"But it was Duke's fault!" insisted Jacob. "He scared Bandit. I want to keep him, Mom. He can't survive on his own. He'll starve!"

I didn't wait for her to respond. "You need to understand something, son: it's illegal to have a wild raccoon for a pet. I can't let you keep him. I'm sorry it has to be this way, but I have no choice."

"What are you going to do with him?" demanded Jacob, his voice breaking as he spoke.

I was hoping he wouldn't ask that question. He put me in a terrible spot because I didn't want to make up a story about how the raccoon would live happily ever after, but I also hated the idea of telling him the truth. "The only way to test an animal for rabies is to take tissue from the brain," I said. "The raccoon will have to be euthanized."

"What's that mean?" he asked.

I paused, looking for the right word. "Put down."

"Down where?"

"He has to be put to sleep, Jacob," said his mother. "There's no other way."

Jacob stared back at her, his face filled with alarm. *"NO!"* he shouted. "I won't let them do that!"

He turned to me, eyes boring into mine. "I hate you!" he cried.

"Jacob!" his mother snapped. "Don't talk to him like—"

He never let her finish. Turning quickly, he ran to the back of the house, tears streaming down his young face. A door slammed. A bedroom I presumed. I could hear him in there, crying like a baby, and my heart sank. Of all my duties as a state game warden, taking an animal from a child is always the most difficult, followed closely by what I had to do next.

Because we don't know how long it takes for raccoon rabies to incubate in humans, the state mandates that they be killed and tested immediately. In the end, Bandit proved negative for the disease, which made my emotions run in two directions: sad that I took an innocent animal's life for nothing, but pleased that Jacob wasn't infected with the dreadful virus.

It is unlawful to take birds and animals from the wild. Most make terrible pets anyway. Wildlife babies might be cute when they're little tykes, but when they mature, most become difficult to handle. This is especially true with raccoons, as they are extraordinarily clever and have the remarkable ability to break into almost any enclosed area. Kitchen drawers, trashcans, and just about all lidded containers and jars are no match for the average adult raccoon. And with front paws similar to human hands, they've even been known to open door latches. Even more problematic is the fact that raccoons can carry a host of harmful parasites that can affect humans, and raccoons are highly susceptible to both distemper and rabies.

Wild birds and animals belong in the wild. Do not try to "rescue" them, most don't need your help, and when you think they're abandoned, it's usually because the mother is hiding nearby, waiting for you to leave so she can be reunited with her offspring. This is especially true with fawn deer.

However, if you come across a baby animal and it's clear that the critter needs your help, you should call your state wildlife agency before acting. Many states have licensed wildlife rehabilitators that know how to look after orphaned birds and animals until they can be released back into the wild where they belong. They are dedicated people who work closely with game wardens to ensure the best possible outcome for our beloved wild creatures.

Published July 1997

And hear the pleasant cuckoo, loud and long –
The simple bird that thinks two notes a song.
   ~W. H. Davis

Cocky

THIS IS A STORY ABOUT A BIRD that had a presumed superiority toward every other creature on the planet, including all two-legged upright beings known as homo sapiens; it's a story about a bird that took the phrase "cock of the walk" as license to bully the entire civilized world into submission, a bird that gave new meaning to the slogan takes a licking and keeps on ticking.

It all began one spring day when the Green family saw a male ring-necked pheasant strutting across their back yard from the kitchen window. The pheasant population in northeastern Pennsylvania had been depressed for as long as they could remember; consequently, they hadn't seen many pheasants on their farm over the years, especially the colorful males, and they hoped the bird would stay awhile, maybe even find a mate.

In an effort to entice the pheasant to stick around, an occasional handful of oats would be tossed out the kitchen window as an incentive, but the pheasant showed no interest in their bribe. Odd they thought, for just about all birds liked oats. But Cocky wasn't like other birds, not by a longshot, and preferred dogfood instead. Every morning, the daft bird would peck leftovers from their dog's bowl as the bewildered hound lay inside his doghouse and watched. And lest you think this feat unremarkable and without audacity, the dog would often express a low growl of contempt from the back of his throat as the feisty bird dined, apparently oblivious to the fact that he could easily become dogfood himself had his canine caterer so chosen.

Cocky also loved tomatoes, which wouldn't have been so bad had he focused on a single tomato now and then. But alas, that wasn't Cocky's style. Instead, he would strut through the garden sampling a dozen or more tomatoes at a time, pecking a single hole into each, thereby ruining them all. And if anyone tried to shoo the crazy cockbird, he'd stand his ground—chest out, feet firmly planted—and reprimand them with an endless string of squawks and cackles, proclaiming the entire tomato patch as his personal property. Anyone who challenged his presumed entitlement would be subject to an immediate assault. Dashing forward with amazing speed, he'd peck at their ankles with his pointy beak in a merciless effort to drive them away before retreating in a zigzag pattern through the field, only to return once again when the coast was clear.

Cocky didn't care much for lawn mowers either. Whenever Mrs. Green would try to cut the grass, the feisty pheasant appeared from out of nowhere and stood directly in front her riding mower, forcing her to drop the transmission into low gear and inch forward while he walked backwards ruffling his feathers and cackling loudly in an attempt to scold the obnoxious machine into submission. One unlucky day he charged directly at it, turning at the last second before being hit by one of the wheels. He managed to survive, but not without losing several tail feathers in the process.

Cocky also went after the Green's huge utility tractor as it mowed their hay fields. He'd run between the wheels, cackling and squawking at the annoying machine in an attempt to drive it away. But when a monstrous wheel clipped him one day and sent him summersaulting into the air, the Greens thought he'd been killed for sure. Although they'd been harassed to the limits by the goofy bird, they'd gotten used to his antics and were deeply saddened by the accident.

But much to their surprise, Cocky strode into to their yard three weeks later looking fit as a fiddle. And although he continued to pilfer food from their dog's bowl and peck holes in their tomatoes, he steered clear of the big tractor from that day on.

Although Cocky tolerated the Green family fairly well, especially Mrs. Green who'd been putting out a generous mixture of grains for the bird in recent weeks, he didn't care much for visitors. So when the local minister stopped by one warm summer day to help out with repairs to their porch, Cocky paced back and forth a few yards away, crowing and cackling at him as he worked. Unfortunately, the preacher was only wearing shorts, and before he could hammer a nail, Cocky lit into him, pummeling his bare legs with his beak until he drew blood. In a knee-jerk reaction, the preacher kicked at him and knocked him several feet backwards. Undeterred, the crazy cockbird came after him again, but when the preacher reached for a two-by-four, Cocky quickly took the hint and retreated into the tomato field.

It wasn't long after, that I received a call from Mrs. Green asking me to take Cocky away. He'd become more troublesome of late, and the attack on their minister was the last straw. Cocky simply had to go.

As I drove to the farm to collect the bird, I thought back on some of the other wildlife complaints I'd received over the years. Nuisance wildlife control was a big part of my job, with troublesome bears topping the list. Beavers were another major source of complaints, as they often flooded county roads and cultivated fields with their dams. Being a trapper all my life, I actually welcomed those calls, putting off the less serious ones until winter when I could supplement my family income with the pelts I collected.

Another major task for Pennsylvania game wardens was the removal of highway-killed deer. I picked up thousands over the years, sometimes as many as a dozen in a single day. I also responded to calls about nuisance squirrels, geese, ducks, turkeys, owls, hawks, rabbits, mink, muskrats, weasels, bobcats, raccoons, bats, foxes, coyotes, otters, opossums, and, last but not least, skunks. But in all my years as a state game warden, this was my first nuisance pheasant complaint.

As I wheeled down the long driveway toward the Green's house, I saw a woman in the distance cutting grass on a riding mower while a pheasant walked backwards in front of her. *Shouldn't be too difficult,* I thought as I pulled up to the house and parked. *The bird looks pretty tame.*

When I exited my vehicle, Mrs. Green shut off the mower and walked over to greet me while Cocky ran into the tomato patch and peeked back at us through the plants.

"He won't fly off when I go after him, will he?" I asked as I pulled a long-handled fish net from the back of my state vehicle.

"Never saw him fly," said Mrs. Green. "I know he can; he has all his feathers. But he usually runs away just out of reach if someone goes after him." She paused and looked over at Cocky hiding among the tomatoes. "I think he knows."

"Kinda looks that way," I said.

"He might let you get close enough to get him with that net if you move slow," she said. "He's real jealous about those tomatoes. Probably won't budge. Thinks they're his personal property."

"Sounds like a plan," I said.

I kept a wary eye on Cocky as I slipped across the driveway with my net. It had a four-foot-long handle with a loop the size of a basketball hoop. I used it to catch nuisance ducks and geese in the past, so I had complete confidence that I'd be able to snag the wayward pheasant with relative ease. But in the heat of the moment, I failed to take in consideration that ducks and geese have webbed feet that are relatively flat, making it difficult for them to move fast on land. Pheasants, on the other hand, have feet built for running on rough terrain, making them much faster and far more nimble than their aquatic cousins.

I was reminded about this the hard way, as once I got close enough to drop the net on Cocky, he did a quick one-eighty and ran through the field. I chased after him, trying not to trample any tomato plants along the way. Unfortunately, I zigged when I should have zagged and fell flat on my face, taking out several plants loaded with ripe tomatoes in the process. Embarrassed, I walked back to Mrs. Green, my ego shattered and my uniform covered with tomato stains.

"There's no way he's going to let me get close enough to catch him," I said, handing her the net. "But you're welcome to give it a try."

She took the net and smiled, her eyes focused on something behind me.

I turned, and there was Cocky standing at the edge of the tomato patch with his head in the air as if gloating in victory, his copper-and-gold plumage iridescent in the blazing sun.

"Okay, I admit it," I shouted. "You beat me!"

Cocky responded by belching out an ear-splitting crow that could be heard a mile away.

I shook my head wearily. "Now he has to tell all the neighbors about it."

Mrs. Green chuckled at my comment. "I hope I have better luck than you did," she said.

"Makes two of us," I told her.

Holding the net behind her back, she started talking softly to the bird as she moved cautiously forward. Cocky turned his head sideways and watched her approach, allowing her to step within a few feet. Then, ever so slowly, she moved the net from behind her, gradually lowering it closer and closer to him until, with one fell swoop, she had him captured.

As Cocky ran in circles inside the net, I went to my patrol car and grabbed a burlap bag. The breathable mesh would give him plenty of air and keep him calm as long as he was covered. It would also protect his feathers, unlike metal cages that wreak havoc on a bird's plumage.

I hustled over to Mrs. Green as she knelt on the ground holding the net over Cocky. After handing her the burlap bag, I dropped to my knees and spread a hand over the pheasant's back and gently pushed him to the ground. Reaching under the net's rim with my other hand, I grasped Cocky by both legs and pulled him out while Mrs. Green held the burlap bag open for me. After dropping him inside, I took the bag and twisted the excess material down toward the bottom until the enclosure wasn't much bigger than Cocky before looping it into a knot. By restricting his movement this way, it would keep him from struggling and reduce the risk of injury.

Mrs. Green accompanied me to my patrol car carrying the net while I cradled the burlap bag in my arms like precious cargo and placed it on the floor by the passenger seat. Then I rolled down the windows so Cocky would get plenty of air and climbed inside.

"Where will you take him?" asked Mrs. Green.

"I know of an abandoned farm," I said. "He'll have plenty of good habitat there."

She sighed heavily. "Gonna miss you, Cocky bird."

Cocky let out a string of mournful chirps at the sound of her voice.

"Better go," I said.

She nodded. Lips pressed tightly, eyes searching mine.

"I'll take good care of him," I said. "Promise."

"I know you will," she said.

I offered a reassuring nod, started my engine and dropped the car into gear. And as I drove down her long driveway toward the state road, I thought I heard her calling me. But it must have been only the wind. For as I watched through my rearview mirror, I saw her slowly turn away and walk back to the house.

Published August 1999

Yours is the Earth and everything that's in it.
And—which is more—you'll be a Man, my son!
   ~Rudyard Kipling

Coalbed Swamp

MY SON FOLLOWED ME INTO THE MINE as I trained my flashlight along its floor of bedrock. Although a small flow of water spilled quietly from the shaft's mouth, we still had enough room to walk along the left wall without getting our feet soaked. The ceiling was low, forcing us to advance hunched over as we made our way into the damp chamber. At about sixty feet, the mine became flooded with underground seepage and we were forced to stop, for the water had swelled across the entire floor.

From here, we could see ribbons of coal running along the stone walls supported by heavy timbers that had remained through the decades. There were several small tunnels carved into the walls where men had once squirmed inside to work on their backs extracting coal deposits deep within, and I wondered what it must have been like to labor here a hundred years ago.

Although the mine was fascinating to see, it was the 140-acre boreal wetland dominated by red spruce—some estimated to be over a hundred years old—that drew us here today, just as it draws some of the most unique wildlife in Pennsylvania. Aptly named Coalbed Swamp, it is part of a complex series of wetlands that includes neighboring Crane Swamp and Tamarack Swamp to the north. We were two miles from the nearest dirt road, atop Dutch Mountain, in State

Game Lands 57. We wanted to explore a bit, hike the old logging trails bordering these wetlands to see what kind of wildlife inhabited the area. I already had a good idea, but it would be all new to my twelve-year-old son, Jesse.

We climbed over the rocky outcropping harboring the coal mine and walked north along a narrow dirt trail hemming the swamp. It wasn't long before we began to see animal tracks. The first belonged to a raccoon. Pretty common fare. But we soon spotted the footprints of a more elusive animal.

"Look at that, Jesse," I said. "Bobcat tracks."

"How do you know?" he asked, stooping for a closer look.

I crouched next to him. "If the tracks were from a canine, like a dog or a coyote, we'd see nail marks," I said. "But cats walk with their claws retracted."

Jesse traced the edge of a footprint with his finger and nodded thoughtfully.

"Canine tracks are more oval, too," I added. "See how round these tracks are? That usually indicates a cat made them. Now look at the heel pads. The front of a bobcat's pad is split into two lobes and the rear is split into three. Canines have one lobe in front and two in the rear."

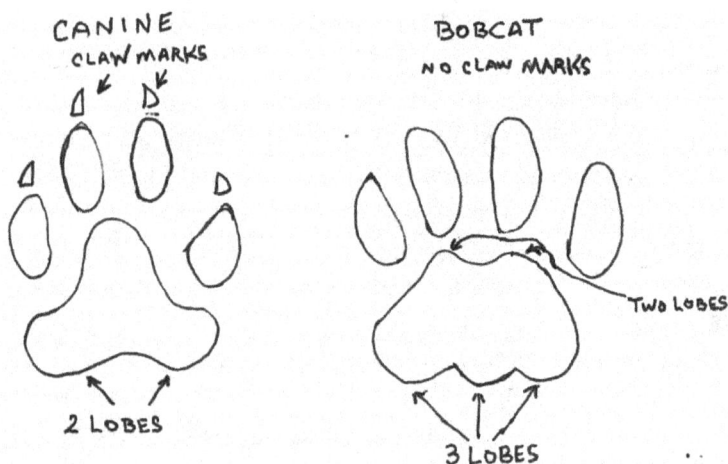

CANINE
CLAW MARKS

2 LOBES

BOBCAT
NO CLAW MARKS

TWO LOBES

3 LOBES

"Do you think we'll see a bobcat today?" asked Jesse.

"Unlikely," I said. "They're nocturnal, but sometimes they come out during the day, especially if they have young to feed. But they prefer hunting at night and have special slit-shaped pupils that let them see in the dark as well as we can see in the daytime."

"That makes them good hunters, right?"

"Sure does."

"Can they kill a deer?"

"They'll kill fawns, but adult deer are tough to bring down, so they don't bother them too often. They usually feed on mice, squirrels, rabbits, and birds like ruffed grouse and turkeys. Most predators go after the easy stuff, Jesse. They're a lot like us and don't want to work any harder than they have to."

Jesse stood and looked over his shoulders into the woods. "Do they attack people?"

"No, they're shy around humans," I said. "Let's keep walking, see what else we can find."

The swamp was thick with laurels, so we veered off to walk along an old bear trail, picking ripe blueberries and eating them as we went. The sky was deep blue and cloudless, the air cool and clean with the branches of oak and maple rustling in the breeze as we walked. It was one of those perfect summer mornings that made you wish every day could be just like this one.

As we moved on, Jesse stopped at every track he found, asking what animal made it. After identifying the track for him, I'd give him a mini-lesson about the critter, just as I had with the bobcat before. We saw the tracks of many different animals, including large bears, some accompanied by the footprints of their cubs.

After we had walked a mile or so, I asked Jesse to identify the tracks we found without my help. He caught on quickly and was able to point out the tracks of coyotes, raccoons, skunks, opossums, foxes, bears and bobcats as we made our way along the trail.

Later, when a grouse flushed right under Jesse's feet, he jumped with surprise.

"What was that?" he gasped

Several more exploded around us, spinning my son in all directions as they rocketed into the woods in twos and threes.

We both laughed out loud after he collected his breath. "You just saw the official Pennsylvania state bird," I said. "They were ruffed grouse!"

"They sure were fast!" exclaimed Jesse. "Do you think more are hiding around here?"

"Might be," I said. "But the population has been low for the past few years. They're cyclic."

"Cyclic?"

"What I mean is the population tends to fluctuate from low to high numbers every five to ten years. We've had a couple bad winters. Grouse don't tolerate harsh weather conditions very well, and their numbers are down. We were lucky to see them today."

Circling south, we made our way back toward our car while listening to the brash chatter of pileated woodpeckers and the rasping croak of a raven somewhere deep in the forest.

We hadn't gone far, when I spotted some fresh droppings in the middle of the trail.

"Coyote!" I remarked.

"How can you tell?" asked Jesse.

He might as well have asked how I know a bulldog when I see one. A bulldog *looks* like a bulldog, just like coyote droppings look like coyote droppings. Plain and simple, right? Maybe for me, but not for my son, and I had to think for a moment before I could explain what made them distinctive.

"Good question, Jesse," I said. "First, they're in the middle of the trail. Coyotes typically mark their territory this way." I stooped by the droppings and motioned him to do the same. "See all the animal hair? That's another indication they're from a coyote. They're about the size of a cigar, too, which makes them too big for fox, and they're pointed at one end, typical for coyote droppings. Looks like this guy was dining on venison; the droppings are full of deer hair."

"Do coyotes kill a lot of deer?" asked Jesse.

"I don't know how many they actually kill, but they do eat a lot of deer. I almost always find deer hair in coyote droppings, especially in the winter. Some are probably road kills and deer lost by hunters. But the bottom line is that coyotes aren't hurting the deer population. We have a lot of coyotes, but we have a lot of deer, too."

I looked at my watch. "It's getting late, Jesse. We better keep moving."

A hundred yards farther down the trail, we spotted another pile of droppings.

"Fox, huh, Dad?" said Jesse.

"That's right. How did you know?"

"They look just like coyote droppings but they're a lot smaller."

And I felt so pleased at that moment. They were the first fox droppings we'd seen that day, and Jesse identified them immediately. Some might think it strange how a father can be joyful over such a such simple thing. But my son reminded me of all the wonderful times I had as a boy following animal sign. And I realized he was experiencing that same joy…that special thrill a youngster feels when he discovers nature and reads sign and knows what creature has visited some remote place before him.

"You've got a good eye, Jesse," I said. "It'll serve you well all through life."

"Thanks, Dad," he said with a proud smile.

I glanced up at the setting sun, then slipped a hand into my back pocket and pulled out a compass. Jesse watched my expression change to a look of concern. "Are we lost?" he asked.

"No, but we're heading in the wrong direction," I said, embarrassed by my mistake. "I thought this trail would be a shortcut, but we need to backtrack for a mile or so. We better pick up the pace."

We turned and followed the trail back some distance until it came to a fork. I checked my compass again and took the south branch, certain we were headed in the right direction this time. After walking another mile, we came to a hunting cabin with a jeep trail leading into it. A good sign to be sure, for we knew the trail had to come from a road. We followed it back and soon came to a narrow dirt lane known as Dutch Mountain Road—the only passage over the mountain.

We still had a three-mile walk to the car, and I could see that Jesse was getting tired. Because the area was remote, and the road seldom traveled, I didn't expect to see any vehicles. But after walking a short distance, a truck rounded the bend from behind and pulled alongside us. It was Vince Hudak, a State Game Lands manager.

"Hey, Bill," he said, a twinkle in his eye. "Who's that you've got with you, a new deputy?"

"You're a welcomed sight, Vince," I said. "This is my son, Jesse."

"Pleased to meet you, Jesse. Helping your dad today?"

"Yes, sir."

"Need a ride, Bill?"

"We sure do," I said gratefully. "We're parked back at the coal mine."

"Well, c'mon, hop in!"

Jesse and I went around to the passenger door and slid inside. Glad to get off my feet for a while, I leaned back and watched the trees and the sky and the clouds drift by as we cruised down the dusty lane toward the coal mine. I glanced at Jesse, asleep in seconds, his head gently on my shoulder. And I closed my eyes and smiled. Content with the feeling that all was right with the world.

Published June 1993

If there is anything that we wish to change in the child, we should first examine it and see whether it is not something that could better be changed in ourselves.
  ~Carl Gustav Jung

The Track of the Poacher

THROUGHOUT MY CAREER, I'VE PROSECUTED more than a few poachers who thought it prudent to bring their children along—to show them the way. This always troubled me because parents should be positive role models for their children and provide strong moral values for them. I can only imagine how demoralizing it must be for a youngster when the game warden strides into deer camp and arrests Dad for a game law violation. I'm not talking about minor infractions— everybody makes mistakes—but rather, premeditated acts like hunting over bait, shooting over the limit, and hunting out of season.

This past deer season my deputies and I investigated nine separate episodes of hunting over bait involving fathers and their sons. One particular incident included two fathers hunting together from neighboring baited treestands with their sons. Both children were only twelve, and it was their first deer hunting experience. They had been counting the days until the season finally arrived, but instead of realizing the thrill and anticipation of the hunt; instead of sharing the camaraderie of a morning with Dad, a man with a badge showed up and hunting was promptly canceled. Unfortunately, the children had to endure the embarrassment of watching their fathers be rousted from their tree stands only to have their firearms seized for evidence and be cited for unlawful hunting.

No sooner had I finished writing their tickets, when I heard four quick gunshots close by. I started through the woods in that general direction and soon came upon an open field where a man and a boy were looking down at two dead deer. Both were holding bolt-action rifles.

"State Game Warden," I called, moving toward them.

They turned, the boy staring at me with owlish eyes as I approached. He looked about the same age as the two I'd just encountered in baited tree stands.

"Who shot the deer?" I asked. Both were does with a limit of one per hunter.

"I did," replied the adult.

"You shot both of them?" I said, making sure I heard him correctly.

"Yeah, my son never fired a shot." He looked down at the two deer and shook his head with regret. "I only meant to kill one of them. The second deer is a mistake."

"How's that?" I asked.

"Well, there were about twenty of them standing here when we walked into them," he said. "They took off right away and I started shooting. Never realized I hit two until they dropped—both at the same time, too. You know how it is, warden. A deer can take a bullet in the heart and run a hundred yards like nothing ever happened."

I said, "If you knew that, maybe you should've been more careful when you started shooting."

He cocked his head and frowned. "What are you saying?"

"I'm saying to shoot repeatedly into a herd of deer on the run and kill two of them is not a mistake. It's negligence. You fired four shots."

"Whoa! Wait a minute here. I didn't do it on purpose!"

I nodded understandingly. "I want to see your hunting license."

He turned, and I removed his cardboard license from the plastic holder pinned to his back and put it in my coat pocket.

"What? I'm gonna get a fine now!" he said.

"You have an illegal kill. Yes, you're going to be fined."

"But that doesn't seem fair!"

"You can take a hearing in front of a judge," I told him. "But for now, I want you to gut both deer, tag the one you want, and follow me back to my car with the other."

"Leave the one I want here?" he said hesitantly.

"You can come back for it when we're finished."

I took both rifles, extracted the magazines, and slung the empty guns over my shoulder while the deer were being unzipped. After both were gutted, they attached a drag rope to the smaller doe and followed me through the woods with it until we reached my patrol car.

I put both rifles on the back seat for safekeeping and then loaded the illegal deer on the big game carrier attached to my rear bumper. After tying it down with rubber bungee cords, I turned and faced them.

"Let me see your hunting license," I said to the boy.

He turned around, and as I removed the license from its plastic holder, a deer tag fell to the ground. The boy's tag was still attached to his license, so I knew it had to belong to someone else. I picked it up and looked it over. "Whose tag is this?" I said.

The boy glanced nervously at his father then back to me. "I...I don't know."

"The number on the tag is only one off from your own license," I said. "And it didn't get tucked in there by itself. Who does it belong to?"

He bowed his head, refusing to answer.

"It's his sister's tag," his father said. "He didn't know it was in there."

"Okay," I said, facing him. "Then, how did it get there?"

He dropped his eyes and shrugged.

"It's illegal to lend your tag to anyone," I said. "Which means your daughter can be fined for this. Do you want me to file charges against her too?"

He shook his head reluctantly. "I don't want her involved," he said. "She doesn't even hunt. I bought a license for her and put the tag in with my son's license. This is all my doing, warden. My kids are innocent."

His admission left little doubt in my mind that the second doe was shot intentionally. And if I had not shown up, the extra tag would have been attached to the deer so it could be transported home as a "legal" kill.

It was disheartening to know that he would willingly rob his children of their innocence by involving them in his own greedy and unlawful behavior. And that stark realization, that feeling of hopelessness for them, made my stomach turn.

I wrote multiple citations for him that day, his fines totaling seven hundred dollars, the maximum at that time. In addition, revocation of his hunting and trapping privileges for at least a year was all but guaranteed.

What our children become in life often hinges on the values and morals we provide as parents. Therefore, we need to show them the path we've chosen in life is on the straight and narrow, a path that leads to honesty, integrity, and proper conduct. For to show your children greed and dishonesty while afield, is to show them the track of the poacher.

Published March 1992

136

It took the whole of Creation
To produce my foot, my each feather:
Now I hold Creation in my foot.
        ~Ted Hughes

Shadow of the Hawk

HAVING NURSED THE THREE TINY NEWBORNS, she covered them in a blanket of grass woven with tufts of downy fur pulled from her belly. Safe now, concealed within the shallow depression she had dug under the wild rose bush, they waited for their mother to return.

The morning sun burned through the remaining bands of nightfall as she left her nest to feed. Moving in short, cautious hops, she paused frequently to watch for anything lurking within the fading gloom. She depended on her sharp hearing to keep her safe, cocking her long ears in every direction while testing the winds with her nose. Her enemies were many, and only through constant vigil would she keep from the clutches of death.

Something moved suddenly in the shadows and she froze instantly, ears flattened against her head. But it was only a dry leaf skipping across the meadow. A depleted remnant of autumn, it rode the gentle spring breeze to infinity and posed no danger to her, so she scampered across the open meadow to a lush patch of clover and began to nibble on the tender shoots.

When she satisfied her hunger, she would return to the protective cover of the wild rose with its dense tangle of thorns. For this was a most dangerous time, out in the open with beasts of prey ever present.

But the constant nursing of her young was exhausting, obliging her to eat a third of her weight daily in order to sustain herself, and a tall patch of broad-leafed weeds tempted her to move deeper into the meadow. The larger plants would satisfy her hunger more quickly, so she took the risk, moving farther from the rose.

Standing on hind legs to reach the succulent leaves, she fed, pausing frequently to watch and listen for signs of danger.

And it was then that she noticed the fierce shadow of the hawk.

Turning quickly, she bolted across the meadow in an unpredictable zigzag pattern to confuse the raptor.

But the hawk, a supreme killer, was familiar with the ploy. It came at lightning speed, so close she could hear the grim whisper of its wings folding behind her.

With more than a thousand prior kills, the red-tail expected to take her effortlessly. But as it was about to crush her with its talons, she cut to the right, her hind end skidding sideways across the dewy grass.

The hawk's feet slammed into the turf, causing the great bird to pitch forward clumsily. But the raptor regained quickly and pulled up, its mighty wings beating frantically. Then it whirled swiftly in the air and came at her for a second and final attack.

But the rabbit had veered off for a reason: a large rock lay just ahead, and she raced for it, pressing her trembling body behind its granite barrier as the giant bird swooped down.

The hawk lifted quickly, then cartwheeled in the air and skimmed over the rock before gliding into the branches of a neighboring oak to rest.

Although protected for the moment, she was still vulnerable. Her instincts told her to run, for the hawk might land close by and walk into her, then snatch her in its claws as she fled.

The red-tail left its perch and let out a mighty scream—a high-pitched *keeeeee-arrr* as it came at her again. Frightened by its terrible cry, she fled across the meadow toward the impenetrable rose. Here she would find safety from the clutches of death, for she knew all secret passages that lay within.

She ran hard and fast. Moving sharply from side to side in an attempt to elude her pursuer, she streaked through the tall patch of broad-leafed weeds and then across the long open meadow, the giant rose bush looming larger with each passing second.

Shelter within its tangled thorns lay just ahead when she heard the hollow thump of wings behind her. She cut to the right in an attempt to get away, but the hawk rolled in the air like a fighter jet and came at her again.

The raptor struck hard, lethal talons penetrating her flesh with mechanical ease as it whisked her off the ground with a single sweeping stroke. And the rabbit stared down at her diminishing world, her body in shock as the hawk climbed a thermal updraft, powerful chest muscles driving its wings in a marvelous fusion of brawn and grace.

Hunting had been difficult for the red-tail with the loss of her mate. A utility cable had broken one of his wings. Unable to fly, he made his way into a briar patch to hide from roving predators. Eventually he starved. It had taken two weeks.

Now there was only one to bring food to the nest, and she would scour the meadows endlessly, the constant search for prey exhausting her.

And as three fledglings crouched in their nest, calling for their mother in high whistling notes, they suddenly saw her black shadow from above. She landed gracefully upon the edge of her nest and gently laid her kill before them. Then, after examining each one carefully, she returned to the skies to hunt once more.

The fledglings ate their fill. And when they finished, they settled comfortably in their massive nest of sticks built high in the branches of a sturdy oak.

Safe now, concealed within its soft depression lined with pine straw and leaves, they waited for their mother to return.

Published August 1992

He was not really bad at heart,
but only rather rude and wild.
~Hilaire Belloc

Terry

HE WAS A LOVABLE LITTLE GUY with his button
nose and crooked left ear. Not a care in the world as he ambled
along the dusty country road on his way to nowhere. It was a
great day with lots of good smells and new places to see. Birds
sang cheerily in the trees above, and a cool breeze ruffled his
curly brown hair, inspiring him to keep moving although the
sun would soon promise a hot and humid afternoon.

It was early September, and Terry, as usual, was exploring
the world on his own. He was a mixed breed, a Heinz if you
will, offering fifty-seven possible varieties of canine ancestry.
His owners were sure about the Terrier strain, but the dog's
remaining genetic makeup had endless possibilities.

Terry had been discovered by chance as he wandered
aimlessly along a rural township road one day. A family of
five, out for a Sunday afternoon ride in the country, almost hit
him with their convertible while rounding a sharp bend. Mom
saw him first.

"Look out!" she cried.

Dad had just turned his head toward a scenic vista but
quickly refocused. He slammed on the brakes and came to a
skidding stop on the dirt road, raising a huge plume of brown
dust around them. This wouldn't have been so bad, except Dad
had insisted on putting the top down earlier. Everyone covered

their faces, coughing and sneezing as they tried to breathe through the powdery haze that blanketed them.

When the dust finally settled, there sat a little dog in the middle of the road, his head cocked inquisitively as he stared up at them with cute little puppy-dog eyes.

"Aww, he's so adorable!" said Mom. "He must be lost."

The children, all three, squealed with glee and begged their parents to take the dog home with them.

And in the end, that's exactly what they did, intending at first to take him to the pound where he'd be adopted by a caring family. But as soon as he got in the car, the loveable pup jumped on the youngest child's lap and started licking her face, his frail body quivering with excitement.

Everyone instantly fell in love with him, so they put an ad in the newspaper's *lost and found* to see if anyone would claim him, and after two weeks when no one came forth, he became a permanent member of their family.

But that was a year ago. Now, with their busy lives in full swing, there was less time to spend with Terry. Every morning he would sit by the front door until someone let him out to do his business. After that, it was out of sight, out of mind. Terry would be free to roam all day long. He'd never known a leash. And why should he, they reasoned. After all, they lived in the country and few cars traveled the narrow dirt roads. Besides, what good was a dog that had to be tied? Dogs were meant to be free, to run and frolic about.

Today was trash day, and much to Terry's delight, most folks put their rubbish in easy-to-open green plastic bags instead of sturdy trashcans. Terry made a beeline straight for them, starting with the next-door neighbor. Here he found three bulging plastic bags along the road at the end of their driveway. He inspected each one, sniffing with his keen nose until he detected food scraps. Then he raked the bag open with his paws and nuzzled through the contents until he found leftovers from last night's dinner. Meatloaf! His favorite.

After wolfing down the chow, Terry scampered off to rummage through the other bags lining the road. It was his favorite day of the week, for they provided the energetic terrier with a virtual smorgasbord of culinary delights.

After eating his fill, Terry dashed into the woods to play. It didn't take long before the trash bags he'd ransacked were spotted by a flock of sharp-eyed crows. They descended like a massive black cloud and picked through the bags with their sturdy beaks, spreading paper scraps, tuna cans, chicken bones and other garbage across the road in a parade of unsightly debris.

Meanwhile, Terry kicked a cottontail rabbit from its hiding place and feigned chase. Too bloated to be a threat, he soon broke off and ambled through the woods in search of easier fare when he came to the wood's edge and padded down a sharp bank that spilled into a roadway. Terry paid no attention to the Chevy sedan heading right for him when he dashed into its path.

The driver, a woman in her early thirties, swerved by reflex and cut the wheel too hard, causing her car to spin violently out of control and plunge down a steep embankment. Rolling once, it slammed into an ancient oak that had stood for a century, the collision so great, every window shattered on impact.

Frightened by the terrible crash, Terry turned and hightailed it back into the woods, oblivious to the tragedy he had caused.

On the following day, the newspaper would report that a young woman had lost control of her vehicle for unknown reasons, leaving behind a loving husband and two small children.

Terry soon found his way to the dirt road that led back to his home. The sight of all the rubbish strewn across the road caused his appetite to return immediately, and he began to search for good smells. But the ravenous crows had cleaned up every last morsel, leaving nothing behind for curious Terrier.

But just as he was about to scamper off, he picked up a strange new scent. It was an animal of some sort, of this he was certain. He knew about rabbits, squirrels and rats, and enjoyed chasing after them, but this…this was something totally different.

A hunter by nature, he put his nose to the wind. It was coming from the wood's edge, and he dashed forward to investigate. There, behind a moss-covered log, a silver-haired bat lay on its back upon the damp forest floor, its feverish body bathed with the pungent sting of guano. Stricken with rabies, the creature grinned at Terry with needle-like teeth as he probed its body with his muzzle, his moist nostrils pulsating over its heady scent.

Although close to death, the bat could still bite, which it did quite suddenly, drawing a tiny bead of blood on the end of Terry's nose. Terry yelped and jumped back, then quickly pounced. Snatching the bat in his mouth, he chewed it into a pulp before swallowing its diseased body whole.

An attractive young woman in her thirties, dressed in shorts and a comfortable cotton blouse, stared intently at the tiny black spots covering her beloved roses. Alarmed, she turned toward the garage for a container of fungicide, snagging her knee on a thorn in the process. It bled well, but it was all part of dealing with her extensive garden. No big deal, really. No big deal at all. On her way for the fungicide, she'd stop at the house to wash off her knee and apply some antiseptic to keep it clean.

That's when Terry appeared at the end of the driveway. He barked twice and bolted playfully toward her.

"C'mon, boy!" she called, clapping her hands excitedly. "Come to Mommy."

Terry scampered down the driveway and raced around her in a series of dizzying circles before dashing over to nuzzle at her legs. Seeing the open wound on her knee, he immediately started to massage it with his tongue.

"Oh, Terry, stop it," she giggled. "Heaven knows what you've been into this morning!"

She gently pushed him back and started toward the house to wash her knee when she changed her mind and turned into the garage for the fungicide instead. Why bother, she reasoned, they say a dog's saliva has wound healing powers, and her loveable little Terry had just licked her knee clean.

Published June 1995

A man who is not afraid of the sea will soon be drowned, he said, for he will be going out on a day he shouldn't.
~ John Millington Synge

The Unprepared

THE WATER SPARKLED AND FLASHED under a blazing July sun as I eased my patrol boat through the still waters of the Susquehanna River. I drifted for a while, floating south under an enormous sapphire sky, in no hurry to spoil the serenity of the day. A huge bass jumped from the waters ahead, its splash sending ripples from bank to bank, and the sudden urge to have a fishing pole in my hands became almost irresistible.

For me, there is no better place on earth than along a lazy river. Its integration of tranquil beauty and raw power have always fascinated me. As in life itself, a river remains peaceful most days, though there will be times of rough water and turbulence ahead. And as in fate, a river is absolute and unforgiving, providing pleasure to those who respect her and death without apology to the foolish and ill-advised.

On this particular day, I was patrolling an area of the Susquehanna known as The Neck, a considerable piece of real estate that juts forth peninsula-like to shove the river around it like a giant elbow. The water is deep here. The fishing superb.

Just ahead, I spotted a boat anchored dead center in the stream. Two middle-aged men were aboard, one sat at the bow, the other at the stern. Each man attended two fishing rods secured to rod holders mounted on the gunwales, their lines cast into deep water. It was time to snap out of my temporary lull. Time to earn my pay, so to speak. I brought my engine to life and eased the boat in their direction.

As I approached, I exchanged greetings with the men. Both had fishing licenses in clear plastic holders pinned to their ball caps, and after a brief inspection of the boat, I didn't see any lifesaving devices (known as personal floatation devices or PFDs), so I asked about them.

"Oh we got 'em," the boat's owner said cheerily. His name was Burt. "They're underneath."

Knowing quick access to a PFD can make the difference between life and death, I asked to see them, explaining that the law requires them to be on deck at arm's reach.

The men exchanged nervous glances. Then Burt instructed his friend at the bow to lift the hinged door on the floor below him. "They're right under your feet, Harry," he said. "Get 'em out for the warden before he gives us a ticket!"

The door was fastened with a barrel bolt latch that had tarnished over the years, requiring Harry to fidget with it before it would slip. When it finally slid free, he pulled open the door and stared down into the hull. "I don't see anything!" he hollered.

"They're right in front of you!" cried Burt. "Reach in and feel around; you'll find them."

I watched in quiet disbelief. *What if Burt had fallen into the river?* I thought. *Would he have time to yell to his friend and explain where the PFDs were stored? And if so, could he get to them in time?*

I doubted it.

Harry got down on his knees and felt around under the deck until he finally retrieved two floatation cushions and pulled them out. "Wish I'd have known about these!" he exclaimed. "They make great cushions, and my butt's been killing me on this wooden seat!"

Burt ignored the comment. "They're Coast Guard approved, warden," he said. "We'll keep 'em up on deck from now on."

Although I appreciated his promise to comply with the law, he still received a citation, and I hoped the ticket would help him remember to have them accessible the next time he was afloat.

I continued downstream and soon came across a boat with seven teenagers aboard. It was obviously overloaded judging by the water it drew. I maneuvered my patrol boat toward them, then shifted into neutral and killed the engine, drifting parallel as everyone on board stared with wide-eyed apprehension.

The first thing I did was check the capacity plate on the transom, which indicated the boat was built for a maximum of four persons.

"Who owns the vessel?" I said.

All eyes went to the teen perched at the stern. He glanced nervously at his friends then back to me. "It's my father's boat," he said. "Not mine."

"What's your name, son?"

"Jimmy," he said. "And my father knows I have the boat."

"Do you have PFDs aboard?"

"Yes, sir," said Jimmy. His eyes cut to the others. "Everybody needs to show the man your safety cushions."

They all pulled cushions from under their bottoms and held them in the air.

"Where's yours?" I asked Jimmy.

"I don't have one."

"Then you'll have to bring the boat ashore."

"You mean right now?"

"Afraid so," I said. "You're one PFD short and your boat is overloaded."

Jimmy's friends groaned with disappointment as he slid across his seat and started the motor. I have to admit, I felt bad for the kids, but there was nothing else I could do. Their safety was my primary concern.

I followed them until they reached the bank, then I handed Jimmy a written warning and told him to keep the vessel out of the water until it conformed to regulations.

"Yes, sir," he said. "Thanks for not giving me a ticket."

I nodded. "Just be more careful next time."

From there, I continued working my way downstream and soon came across two men fishing from a boat anchored midstream. I pulled aside and struck a casual conversation with them. Their fishing licenses were in order, their bass were all legal, and they had PFDs on the floor next to them, so I soon departed.

But voices carry over calm waters as freely as an egret glides. And I overheard one man crack that he was glad he'd stowed the PFDs after thinking about leaving them home.

I guess he didn't understand.

Having proper life saving devices aboard and within reach isn't about beating the game warden. It's about beating the river. It's about returning home to your wife, kids, friends, dog, parrot, or whomever it is you love... and loves you back.

It's about life, my friends. Life!

Published September 1999

We're eyeball to eyeball, and I think the other fellow just blinked.
    ~ Dean Rusk

Unlawful Attempt

"THERE'S SOMEONE HUNTING OVER BAIT up here!" the man blurted over the phone. He was fuming mad. "I put feed out for turkeys all year long, and somebody parked his truck near my house and went back into the woods with a rifle! I need you to come out here and get this guy!"

The sun was just starting to peek over the mountains, and I was on my way out the door when I got the call.

"You caught me just in time," I said. "Give me an address and I'll be right over."

The complainant lived in Forkston, a twenty-minute ride. I hung up and slipped out the back door, hoping the early morning call hadn't awakened my wife and two young children.

My patrol car was parked at the top of my driveway facing the road. I jumped inside, keyed the ignition, and made my way toward Forkston at a good clip. It was the last day of doe season, and I figured the hunter was probably after deer, not turkeys.

Six inches of fresh snow covered the ground as I steered off the main highway onto a dead-end township road. It was plowed clear until it turned into a private lane a hundred yards ahead. Here it became a snowy two-track that continued uphill through the woods to the complainant's house some distance away. The hunter had parked his truck at the bottom of the hill and walked from here, so I shifted into four-wheel-drive and followed him up toward the house.

Halfway to the top, I saw someone peering at me from behind a pine tree off to my right. He was dressed in orange, a good fifty yards away, and as soon as I stopped my car, he ducked out of sight.

The chase was on, so I shut down the engine, set the brake, and raced after him on foot. Six inches of snow isn't all that much, but coupled with my winter coat, heavy gun belt and clumsy leather boots, it didn't take long before I started to get winded and slowed to a walk.

The air was clear and cold as I followed his trail through the snow. The long stride of his tracks told me he had started off running, but the distance between his boot prints soon shortened as he slowed to a walk. After all, he was weighted down about as much as I was with his hunting coat, boots and rifle.

He headed north at first, probably in a frantic attempt to distance himself as fast as possible. But he soon changed his mind and circled south toward his truck at the base of the hill, so I stepped up my pace, hoping to catch him before he reached his vehicle. My eyes bored into the woods as I pushed ahead. I had no idea what he was capable of or what he might be thinking, and I didn't want to be the victim of an ambush by some panic-stricken fool.

Suddenly I saw him a mere hundred feet ahead. He stepped from behind an oak tree and faced me, his rifle cradled across his chest.

I stopped and canted my body at a forty-five degree angle to offer a smaller target. "State Game Warden!" I called, palming my .357 magnum. "Lean your gun against the tree and step away from it."

He complied immediately. Setting the rifle's stock into the snow, he leaned the barrel against the oak and kept his hands at his side. He was in his early twenties with a narrow face and nervous eyes that constantly flicked left and right as if watching for some unseen assailant.

"Why did you run away?" I said, walking up to him.

"I thought you were the landowner," he said. "I don't have permission to be here."

It was a lie, but I let it go. My patrol car was clearly marked. He had to see the state emblem on the door and the emergency lightbar on the roof.

I took his rifle from the tree and checked the magazine and chamber. Both were empty. "Where's your ammunition?" I said.

He dug into his coat pockets, extracted six .30-06 caliber bullets and held them out. "I'm not hunting." He said. "I was just looking around. Honest."

I took the ammo from him, pocketed it, and asked to see his hunting license.

He did an about-face, and I removed the cardboard license from the plastic holder pinned to the center of his back. There was no doe tag attached. "I see you already got one," I said.

"Last October with my bow. But like I said, I'm not hunting. Just taking a walk, looking around."

I stuffed his hunting license in my pocket and eyed him critically. "Let me get this straight," I said. "You're in the middle of the woods, a half-mile from nowhere, on the last day of doe season, with a rifle in your hands. There are deer tracks all over the snow, you're dressed in full orange, and you have a hunting license on your back. Do you really expect me to believe you're not hunting?"

"You checked my gun," he said defensively. "It wasn't loaded."

It never ceased to amaze me how many ridiculous excuses people could think of when they were caught breaking the law. Most believed they could get away scot-free as long as I didn't actually see them commit the crime. But game wardens, just like all police officers, can prosecute suspects based solely on circumstantial evidence. We do it all the time. And we win convictions in courts more often than not.

A game warden can prove guilt in a court of law through either direct or circumstantial evidence, sometimes a combination of both. An example of direct evidence would be when an eyewitness appears in court to testify that he saw someone shoot a deer in closed season. Circumstantial evidence, however, is evidence that leads to the conclusion that a crime was committed even though there is no witness testimony—as in the case at hand, where a suspect is found in the woods wearing a hunting license with a high-caliber rifle during doe season and runs from the game warden.

I shouldered the man's rifle and directed him to start walking back to my patrol car with me.

"Am I under arrest?" he asked.

"Consider it detainment for now," I said. "When we get back to my vehicle, I'm going to cite you for attempting to kill a doe in closed season."

"But I didn't even shoot my gun! How can I be fined for attempting to kill anything?"

"Trust me. You can. Take a hearing if you want; tell your story to the judge. See if he believes you. Now, let's go."

When we got back to my vehicle, I slid inside and grabbed my citation pad. But I left the door open as I wrote, and from the corner of my eye, I saw him shuffling toward me. When he reached the door, he said, "You were right, officer." His face had turned grim, lips pressed into a frown.

I set my pen down and looked at him. "Beg pardon?"

"You were right all along," he said. "I was hunting. I won't go to court and lie. I just want to pay the fine and get it over with."

"Hunting what?" I asked.

He shrugged. "Deer. It's the last day, and I wanted to see if I could get one."

Although he claimed he didn't want to go to court, I wasn't so sure. Poachers have told me that before, then they go home and talk to some barroom attorney who convinces them to take a hearing and the case ends up in court anyway. But the fact that he'd just admitted to hunting would weigh heavily against him if he changed his mind and decided to take the matter before a judge.

"How much is the fine, anyway?" he asked.

"Five hundred dollars."

He was stunned. "Oh man!" he gasped. "That's a lot of money!"

"It's supposed to be," I said. "We try to make it a deterrent."

"Will I lose my license for this? I really love to hunt."

"That's not up to me," I said. "The front office makes that decision. But I think you probably will."

The same old story, I thought. Every season we have people who brag to their buddies about how many deer they kill and how they've never been caught. It's like a game to some. And for years, they get away with it. Then, finally, they're apprehended and the penalty staggers them.

Game wardens constitute but a thin green line between the lawful hunter and willful violator; consequently, unscrupulous hunters often manage to slip through our defense system of dedicated enforcement officers. Honorable hunters can help by acting as the eyes and ears of the wildlife officer and report game law violators when they see them. Only by working together can we hope to preserve our hunting and trapping heritage, not only for our children, but for future generations to come.

Published March 1996

I love cats. They taste just like chicken.
~Unknown

Dogs, Cats, and Automobiles

I WAS DRIVING HOME THE OTHER NIGHT when I almost hit an orange cat as it darted in front of my car before vanishing into the woods for its nightly killing spree.

I'd seen that mouser before. Even knew whose house it belonged to. Obviously well fed, its paunch swayed prominently to and fro whenever I'd see it prowling my neighborhood—which was far too often. Unfortunately, a bellyful of cat chow seldom quells the urge to hunt in housecats. They kill for fun, not food.

By now you probably think I'm about to launch into another tirade about cats, but rest assured, dear reader, I am not. In fact, you might be surprised to know I've owned two cats before. The first was a gray kitten that my brother, John and I found when we were kids. It was a warm June day, and we were fishing along the Neshaminy Creek in Warminster, Pennsylvania when we heard a series of frantic mews coming from somewhere close by. Reeling in our lines, we followed the cries to a culvert pipe that ran along the road's edge a short distance away.

We knelt by the mouth of the culvert to peek inside, and a tiny kitten scurried out to greet us. Crying and miserable and apparently abandoned, I picked up the cat and held it against my chest, its cries soon melting into soft purrs of blissful content.

"Cute little thing," said my brother as he reached over and massaged its head. "It must be starving; let's take it home and give it something to eat."

We had a pet boxer at the house, so I hesitated at first. "What about Champ?" I said. "He might hurt it."

"Not if you're holding on to it like right now," insisted John. "Let him sniff it a little; he might even *like* a new friend."

"Good idea," I said.

"I think Mom will let us keep it," my brother added. "She loves cats."

I looked down at the kitten as it licked my fingers with its sandpapery tongue. I could feel its heart beating in my hands. There was no way I could abandon it.

"Let's go ask her," I said. "We'll give it some milk, too."

We brought the kitten home, and my mother, as suspected, immediately fell in love with it. But we thought it best not to tell Dad right away. He worked long hours in downtown Philadelphia every day, and Mom didn't think he'd want to find a cat in the house when he walked through the front door that night. So we decided to keep our kitten a secret for a few days and gradually introduce him to the idea. But the days turned into weeks, and we still hadn't told him about it, when one Sunday afternoon he heard it crying in the garage. We had no choice. We had to fess up. But to our surprise and delight, Dad took a liking to the kitten right away, and it became a permanent member of our family, living a long and healthy life.

But the orange cat at the beginning of this story is what prompted me to write this. For it reminded me of an incident that happened many years ago when I actually did run over a cat with my automobile.

I was on my way home from a construction job when a little orange kitten bolted out of a field bordering the highway and dropped into a trembling ball of fur directly in front of my car. Cruising along at sixty, there was no way I could stop in time, so I aimed for the cat dead center, its eyes peeking up at me as I ran over it with my '62 Oldsmobile.

VAROOOOOM!

Hoping three thousand pounds of barreling steel hadn't flattened the tiny critter into an orange Frisbee with whiskers, I checked my rearview mirror and saw the kitten still crouched in the middle of the street. Deeper in the mirror, I could see a hail of shiny automobiles looming in the horizon, and they were coming fast. There was no way the kitten would survive.

I came to a screeching stop, jammed the Olds into reverse, and decked the accelerator, racing backwards along the berm until I came alongside the kitten and hit the brakes. I took a quick peek over my shoulder. The tangle of traffic was almost on us, and since I'd already saved its hide once, I wasn't about to let it be ground into the pavement. With seconds to spare, I dashed onto the highway and snatched the helpless kitten from certain death.

Moments later, as I sat in my Oldsmobile listening to the steady whoosh of traffic sail by, I wondered what I should do with the kitten as it looked up at me with its big green eyes. It was November, and it was cold outside, and the poor thing was shivering and probably half starved. Likely born under a junked car in the neighboring field, its coat was streaked black with grime. Feral to be sure, it had no place to call home, and I simply couldn't bring myself to abandon it. My hunting boots lay on the floor by the passenger seat, so I plopped the kitten inside one of them and drove straight home.

"Honey, look what I found!"

My wife, Maryann, fell in love with it immediately. But the kitten was wild and afraid, so we kept it in our basement along with some fresh food and water and a tray of sand for a toilet. For weeks, it lived under the furnace, refusing to come near us. But eventually, with patience and coaxing, Maryann was able to feed the kitten by hand. She named it Kittron, and eventually it became a regular member of our family.

Kittron grew into a pretty decent cat, too. We kept her indoors and had her spayed. And although we provided a scratching post to keep her from clawing our belongings, she rarely used it and never touched our furniture.

I have to admit, I really liked that cat. She was intelligent, affectionate, and well behaved, almost as well behaved as a dog. And she had a personality of sorts. It was as if she could read our minds at times. But one day she began having trouble with her bowels and started leaving unwelcomed packages around the house. We took her to a veterinarian, hoping to find a way to help her, but there was no cure, and the vet suggested we keep her outside.

My first reaction was a resounding no. I've always been against allowing cats to roam free. But my only other choice was to put her down, and I just couldn't do that to a cat whose life I'd saved just a few years earlier.

So, after a lot of soul searching, I decided to let her stay outside as long as she didn't kill any wildlife. My biggest concern was that she might get run over by a car, but when I saw her stop at the edge of our property one day and look left and right before crossing the street, I was convinced she was going to be okay. Kittron was a very smart cat.

I watched her closely for several months, and to my delight, I never found a single dead bird or animal on our property. Kittron was well fed, but what's more, she was on the lazy side, and I guess she simply couldn't be bothered chasing after lesser critters.

As winter approached, I took some of the split wood I had stacked for the fireplace and built a small cubby (a log cabin of sorts) under our roofed front porch. It was just big enough for her to squeeze into and had a low ceiling to help hold her body heat on cold winter nights. She loved it!

Everything seemed to be working out just fine until new neighbors moved in next door. They had a dog named Foxy. Foxy barked a lot whenever he was tied out back, so his owners would often let him run free. Then Foxy would come over to our yard, deposit a smoking-hot stool on our front lawn, and start looking for Kittron.

Dogs love to chase cats. After all, it's what they do, right?

Kittron would hide in our shrubbery when she saw him coming, but Foxy would find her anyway. Dogs have a great sense of smell. They'll find you every time. And when Foxy found Kittron, she would run into the culvert pipe at the end of our property to hide. There she would be safe, for Foxy was too big to fit inside.

One day, eight years after I had saved her life, Foxy came into our yard and chased Kittron into the street. Only this time she didn't look both ways.

Days later, I discovered her bloated body lying by the mouth of the culvert. She'd been hit by a car and was trying to get to the one place that made her feel safe. It was a sad day, finding her like that. A day I remember all too well, though more than twenty years have passed.

Published February 1994

The Fawn

June 1989

"LOOK MOMMY, LOOK! A BABY DEER!"

The eight-year-old twin girls had unbuckled their seatbelts and were jumping up and down on the back seat, pointing into the field on their right. Fearing for their safety, their mother pulled to the berm and stopped the car.

She spotted the fawn immediately. It was curled into a tight circle just off the road, its reddish-brown coat, dotted with vivid white spots, stood out like a beacon in the grassy field.

"Aww, the poor thing," said their mother. "It must have been abandoned."

"Can we keep it!" the girls cried in chorus. "It's so cute! Please, can we?"

"I don't know about that," their mother cautioned. "A baby deer takes a lot of looking after."

"Please, Mommy, please! We'll name it Bambi and everything!"

She turned and looked into their pleading faces. The past year had been difficult with the death of their father, and she hated the idea of disappointing them. Besides, the deer was obviously abandoned and would die if they didn't do something, and she certainly didn't want *that* terrible thought preying on their minds.

"Well…I suppose we can't just leave it here," she said.

The fawn watched curiously as three strange creatures spilled from the belly of the giant metal beast and moved toward him. Strange indeed, they walked upright on two legs. A mother with two young females, he sensed, just as he too had a mother and was young. Instinctively, he lay tight to the ground, motionless save the rhythmic flair of his nostrils as he took in their scent.

One stumbled and fell as they approached. She uttered an unfamiliar, high-pitched cry as her mother ran to her. The other continued to come forward until she knelt by his side and stroked his head with soft, naked fingers. Ever so carefully, she slipped two arms under his folded legs and held him to her chest. She was warm and soft, and he could feel the rapid beating of her heart. The encounter was gentle, and so he remained docile, for his mother was gone and he longed for companionship.

Her twin sister and her mother watched as she walked toward them with the delicate baby deer cradled in her arms. It was licking her perspiring neck for the minerals excreted in her sweat, and this sealed his fate, for they were convinced the fawn was offering its affection for saving its life. So it was with profound glee that they placed him on the back seat of their car where he settled into a snug circle between adoring twin girls.

In the woods, fifty yards away, the fawn's mother and his twin remained hidden. They had run off when the metal beast approached and were waiting for him to join them, but he had lost his mother's scent and lay curled in the field to hide. Had he been in the forest, his coat would have blended with the surrounding shadows, but in the grass, he was easily detected.

Now they watched helplessly as the beast swallowed him, then roared to life and vanished in the dust created within its wake.

And he was gone.

November 1992

The huge buck stood alone in his meager steel-wire pen. As a fawn, the cage seemed large to him. But now the eight-foot-square enclosure had become a confined and dismal prison. Rutting season was in, and with his hormones at peak level, he was in continuous discomfort with his solitude.

Twin girls who used to visit him every day, walk by his cage on their way to school each morning without a glance his way.

He saw them coming today and stood watching. As they neared, one dropped her books clumsily on the ground. It was the same twin who stumbled and fell the day he was taken. The one who had cried. The weak one. This he knew, for some innate sixth sense enabled him to tell them apart. Everyone else, with the exception of their mother, found it impossible.

Both girls stooped to gather the scattering of books, and when they stood, found themselves mere inches from his cage. A massive twelve-point buck, his chestnut eyes boring into them. Frightened by his menacing stare, the girls quickly ran off to school.

Later that afternoon, when the twins returned home with a girlfriend, the buck stood in his bleak cage and watched as they approached.

162

"Oh look!" cried their friend. "A deer! I didn't know you owned a deer! He's so beautiful! What's his name?"

"Bambi," the twins replied simultaneously, proud that their friend envied them.

"That is so cool!" she squealed. "I love him!"

"We had him since he was a baby," said one twin.

"His mother abandoned him, so we had to save his life," added the other.

"Aww, that is so sweet! May I pet him?"

"He's pretty big," they cautioned. "I don't know if that's a good idea."

"Oh, please! Just for a second. Please, may I?"

She was the president of Student Council and very popular in school, and so the twins, not wanting to jeopardize their new friendship, gave in to her. "Okay," they told her. "But only for a minute."

The buck sensed what was about to happen and moved back, his muscular body statue-like as the twins worked the latch on his cage.

When they opened the door for their friend, she marched inside eager and unafraid. And as she reached out to stroke the buck's heavy neck, he bolted, his hardened body slamming her against a corner-post, fracturing three of her ribs as he fled.

As the twins raced toward their house, screaming for their mother, one fell to the ground and cried. Had the buck still been in his cage, he would have known it was the same one who had stumbled and fallen the day he was taken.

But he was free now. Finally, he was free.

Published November 1995

I had a dream that was not all a dream.
~George Noel Gordon
Darkness

The Return

AS I WRITE, SNOW IS FALLING in tiny frenzied flakes. The first significant snow of the season. The sky is slate gray and the white powder is piling up fast. There must be eight inches on the ground already. It reminds me of last winter when the deep snows lingered well into spring. And Beauford first appeared in my dreams.

I never intended to tell this story and can't understand why I suddenly feel compelled to now. It's just that it's snowing and everything is so white and this uncontrollable urge has suddenly come over me. My fingers are dancing across the keys of my word processor, spilling out sentences as if the machine had a mind of its own. It's the snow I say. It makes everything so hushed. So tranquil...like in dreams.

Ohio is a long way from home. As most of you know, it was there that I had some rather serious surgery last summer. I was also given some rather serious drugs to kill the pain. That, my friends, is why I have to wonder if what I'm about to tell you ever occurred, especially since I've been told hallucinations are common with heavy painkillers.

It all started with the morphine. My wife warned them not to give it to me because my brother had a bad reaction to it seven years earlier with the same surgery.

But they didn't listen.

I remember a nurse waking me late at night as she hurriedly disconnected the plastic tube pumping the medication into my veins. I didn't know it then, but my respiration had plummeted to only five breaths per minute. The nurse gave me a quick shot of Narcan to reverse the effect of the morphine and then stepped back.

That was when my guts began to heave into an agonizing knot. I curled into a fetal position, shivering wildly, my teeth chattering so fiercely I thought they might crack. Three women, their uniforms white as snow, scurried into the room and began throwing blankets over me. I saw their eyes narrow grimly, and fear swarmed into my heart. Then everything around me began to spin, and darkness fell over me like a veil…

…Hey big guy, don't let go!

A voice clear as day. Its terse, matter-of-fact tone familiar, but I couldn't quite place it. My eyes snapped open, the moonlight filtering into my room through a window behind me. In its cold glow, I could see the faint silhouette of a rabbit sitting at the end of my bed.

"Beauford!" I marveled.

You sound pleased to see me again. I'm touched. Sorry I can't stay. Just stopped by to check on you.

At the time it all seemed perfectly normal to me—my conversation with a rabbit, that is. "I'm surprised to see you," I said. "And you're right. I am pleased."

Had a rough time of it a little earlier, didn't you.

"I don't remember much about it," I said. "I must have blacked out."

It was bad. Take my word for it. I wouldn't have made the trip otherwise. By the way, what are they feeding the squirrels around here? They're big as housecats!

"They're fox squirrels, Beauford. You're used to their smaller cousins, gray squirrels—but tell me, why are you here, really? I didn't think I'd ever see you again."

Know how a rabbit's foot is supposed to be good luck? Well, you looked like you needed more than just the foot.

"In that case, thanks for coming," I said.

165

Pretty gross superstition if you ask me, anyway.

"I have to agree," I said truthfully. "By the way, you look pretty good since your tangle with the cat last winter. You're not blind anymore and your one ear grew back. How'd that happen?"

C'mon, Bill, wake up. No, wait! I take that back (Beauford chuckles nervously). *Speaking of looks, you don't look so good yourself, partner. The surgery must have taken a lot out of you.*

"Very funny," I said. "You know what they did to me!"

Okay, bad joke. Sorry.

"Don't try to change the subject, Beauford. Your left eye was gone and your ear was chewed off the last time I saw you. You were covered with blood...dying. Something weird is going on here!"

Weird! Like what? The fact that you're having a conversation with a rabbit and it's just starting to dawn on you that rabbits CAN'T TALK! You mean weird like that? In that case, you'd better not quit your day job, big guy. And I'd forget about working for NASA in the future, too.

"You're right," I said. "This isn't really happening. It can't be! You're not real. It's just my imagination playing tricks on me. Tricks...that's all. Just tricks..."

"Sir, wake up!"

My eyes opened, blinking slowly, and I saw the nurse that had given me the Narcan standing over me with a paper cup in her hand.

"Time to take your medicine," she said, handing me the cup.

I drank the goop inside and handed it back. "I was having a dream," I said.

"I know," she assured me. "You were talking in your sleep. It's the medication. You'll be fine."

"What time is it?" I asked.

She checked her wristwatch. "Three o'clock."

"I knew it."

166

"Excuse me?"

"Never mind," I said. "Earlier, when you gave me the shot and I had the cramps and chills...I must have had a bad reaction from the morphine, huh?"

"Yes," she said. "But I still don't know how you managed to buzz me. You were out cold."

"Buzz you?"

"Yes. I came right in and saw your breathing was...well, wasn't right. That's when I gave you the shot...to bring you back."

"I didn't push any buzzer," I said.

The nurse stared at me in genuine puzzlement. "Well, *somebody* must have."

"Where is it anyway?" I said, lifting my covers to look.

She walked to the opposite side of my bed, then stooped and picked up a white plastic box dangling on its cord. "Well, you couldn't have rolled on it and set it off by accident," she said, handing it to me. "Just push the red button if you need me again."

And then she did something that haunts me to this day. As she was about to walk out the door, she turned, and I saw a shrewd smile flash across her face as if she knew something secret and special.

"You must have a guardian angel looking over you," she said with a wink. Then she stepped out of the room and disappeared into the hall.

Published January 1994

167

"We be one blood, thou and I," Mowgli answered. *"I take my life from thee tonight. My kill shall be thy kill if ever though art hungry, O Kaa."*
~Rudyard Kipling
The Jungle Book

Blood

DNA **PROFILING RECEIVED WIDE ATTENTION** in the news media in 1994 when it came into the national spotlight during the O.J. Simpson murder trial, described as the most publicized criminal trial in American history. Live courtroom testimony, based largely around DNA evidence, was televised for one hundred thirty-five days, turning countless viewers into Simpson trial fanatics. I still remember his picture on the cover of *Newsweek* with the caption "TRAIL OF BLOOD" printed across his chest in huge red letters. Blood traces were found at the crime scene and many pundits claimed the DNA evidence against Mr. Simpson was overwhelming. One forensic scientist stated that the blood evidence presented in the case was so exacting it eliminated practically the entire human population and that it could only have come from Mr. Simpson or his identical twin (if he had one).

Perhaps that's what motivated State Game Warden John Wasserman when he found a bloody knife in the hands of a suspected poacher that very same year. Up until then, DNA profiling had never been used on a poaching case in Pennsylvania. But then, if two concerned sportsmen hadn't gotten involved, there wouldn't have been any case in the first place. The story goes as follows.

Veto and Dominick were driving through a remote section of Clinton County in northcentral Pennsylvania when they saw two men dragging a deer across a graveyard in the dark of night.

"Look over there!" said Veto. "They've got a deer down!"

As he brought his pickup truck to a stop, the two men dropped the deer and froze in their tracks. They stood a mere thirty yards away, black statues under a vivid full moon.

"I don't see horns on that deer," said Veto. "I'll bet it's a doe."

"One way to find out," said Dominick. Then he opened the passenger door and started to get out.

When the two men saw the door pop open they took off in opposite directions, one running into the woods by the cemetery while the other ran directly in front of Veto's headlights before disappearing into the night.

Certain the men were poachers, Veto and Dominick jumped out of the truck and hustled over to the deer.

"A doe," grunted Dominick. "I knew it!"

"I'll bet they came from one of the cabins we just passed along the road," said Veto.

"I think you're right," said Dominick. "They didn't even have coats on, and it's freezing outside."

He knelt by the gutted carcass and slipped his hand under a front leg. "Still warm," he said, looking up at Veto. "They might come back for it."

Veto nodded in agreement. "Renovo is about ten miles from here. Let's head down and call for a game warden."

"You go," said Dominick. "I'm going to wait here for them."

Veto frowned with concern. "Alone? There's two of them, and they might be armed."

"I'll hide someplace where no one can see me," said Dominick. He reached into his coat pocket and pulled out a

small-caliber handgun. "If there's trouble, I'll be ready for it."
Then he shoved the gun back into his coat and gave Veto an
impatient look. "You better get going before somebody sees
your truck and thinks *we* killed the deer."

"Okay. Just be careful."

"I will. Now, get out of here."

Veto jogged back to his Dodge Ram and climbed inside.
He looked back at his friend as the engine came to life, then
he dropped the truck into gear, cranked the steering wheel for
a tight U-turn, and sped back down the mountain road toward
town.

State Game Warden John Wasserman just sat down to dinner
when the wall phone rang behind him. The December buck
season was in full swing and had him running double shifts
every day for the past two weeks. He was tired and hungry and
thought about letting it ring for once. Instead, he rose from the
table and picked up the receiver just as he had a thousand
times before.

Ten minutes later, he was heading up Tamarack Mountain
Road in his marked patrol vehicle. *Dead deer in a graveyard,*
he thought. *Imagine that...*

When John reached the cemetery, he saw a silver Dodge
Ram parked just off the road and pulled behind it. He stopped
approximately one car-length away and slightly off-center, his
high beams illuminating the truck. Then he turned on his
spotlight, directing the beam into the cab through the truck's
rear window where he saw the silhouettes of two occupants
inside. He picked up his mic and called in the license plate
along with his location as a precaution. Although he knew the
truck belonged to the man who had just called about the deer,
there was always the possibility of a setup. Someone who
wanted to lure him into this remote location to harm him for
some imagined past grievance. As a game warden for more
than twenty years, he had many arrests under his belt. Some
poachers had vowed to get even. Most were just blowing

smoke, but there were others who were more than capable of keeping their word.

John exited his state issued green Chevy Blazer and started toward the Dodge, staying alert for suspicious movements from inside. He was in full uniform with his felt campaign hat tilted down at a slight angle, leather chinstrap tucked just below his lower lip.

As he drew near, the driver began to open his door. John froze and immediately warned him to stay inside, knowing the bright lights from his vehicle would be to his advantage if things went south. The driver complied, and John moved forward once again, stopping just outside his open window. He shined his flashlight into the cab. Both men were in their mid-twenties and dressed in camouflage hunting clothes. He'd never seen them before.

"Officer Wasserman?" asked the driver.

"Yes."

"I'm Veto," he said, squinting through the glare of light from John's patrol car. He nodded toward his passenger. "This is my friend, Dominick."

"Thanks for coming here tonight," said John.

"No problem, officer."

"You can both step out now. I'll kill my lights and we'll go take a look at the deer."

Veto and Dominick slid out of the Dodge Ram and stood by the tailgate while John shut down his Blazer and tossed his campaign hat on the passenger seat, replacing it with a more comfortable uniform ball cap. Then he walked back to the men with his handheld flashlight and followed them into the cemetery.

The doe was a six-month-old fawn, shot with what appeared to be a thirty-caliber bullet. The slug had entered its head on the left side, taking out a portion of its skull and brains on exit. There was no gut pile nearby, indicating it was likely shot back in the woods someplace and hidden until the poachers could retrieve it under the cover of darkness. It was by dumb luck they were discovered while dragging it through the cemetery, which, John thought, seemed to be the way most poaching cases were exposed…that is, by dumb luck.

"Nobody saw a truck parked anywhere, right?" John asked.

"That's right," said Dominick. "We think they have a camp nearby because they weren't wearing coats. No rifles either."

"Get a good look at them?"

"One of 'em," said Veto. "He ran in front of my headlights. Pretty big guy. He was wearing a red shirt. The other one took off into the woods at the back of the cemetery. He was too far away to get a good look. He had a full beard; that's all I can tell you."

John turned to Dominick. "See any vehicles come by while you were here?"

"Nope, not a one."

"You're probably right about the camp being nearby," said John. "My guess is they were dropped off, expecting to be picked up later with the deer. Then you two came along and spoiled their plans."

"So now what happens?" asked Dominick.

"I'm going to wait and see if they come back," John said. "There's a camp just down the road that's not being used this season. It'll be a good place to hide my vehicle."

"How 'bout we follow you down and wait until you're ready to call it quits," said Veto. "You might need some help."

John hesitated. It was an unusual proposal.

Veto saw the doubt in his face. "I know what you're thinking," he said. "But if you catch the guy, you're gonna need somebody to identify him. And we're the only ones that can do that."

Hours passed and the temperature had plummeted as John waited behind a large pine tree at the edge of the cemetery. His feet were blocks of ice, and he tapped his boots together and stomped on the ground to help ward off the numbing cold. He took a protein bar from his coat pocket, unwrapped it and chewed hungrily, glad he'd remembered to bring something along after missing his dinner. The bar was coated in chocolate, his favorite. And it would go well with some hot coffee. He grabbed his Stanley thermos and squeaked open the rubber stopper. The steaming liquid gurgled into his cup, and after pouring, he wrapped both hands around it hoping to draw in a few Btu's.

But as he brought the cup to his lips, he caught a shadow from the corner of his eye. In the short time it had taken him to pour his coffee, someone had stepped noiselessly by, almost slipping out of sight on the dark country road. John dumped the coffee and sprinted through the cemetery, dodging gravestones as he went. Rounding a hundred yards in a matter of seconds, he soon reached the road. The man hadn't gotten far, his profile illumined in the moonlight as he shuffled along, unaware that John was behind him.

"State Game Warden! Hold up!"

The man froze at the sound of John's voice, then spun around to face him. He was in his early thirties with the protruding forehead of a Neanderthal. His deep-set eyes, high cheekbones and fierce beard made him look even more primitive. John palmed the butt of his .357 Magnum revolver, his flashlight pointing at the suspect's midsection, revealing his hands and beltline. He appeared to be unarmed, but John needed to be certain. He ordered the man to turn around and place his hands behind his head, interlocking his fingers. Then he had him drop to his knees. He had no coat, the seat of his pants damp, as if he'd been sitting outside for a while. Keeping his light focused on his suspect, he retrieved his handcuffs and hooked him up, hands behind his back. Then he brought him to his feet and patted him down for weapons. Satisfied he was unarmed, he asked for a name.

"Jason Platt," the man replied angrily. "What's going on, man? I didn't do nothing!"

John trained his flashlight on his suspect's hands and clothing looking for deer hairs or bloodstains that might link him to the illegal doe, but he found nothing.

"Where are you from?" asked John."

"Philly," he said. "What's this all about?"

"I have two witnesses that saw someone matching your description with an illegal deer earlier tonight."

"That's crazy!" he grunted. "I didn't kill no deer."

"They saw you with another man dragging it through the cemetery."

"Then your witnesses better get their glasses fixed. I was just coming back from the bar. Heading to my camp. I don't know nothing about a deer."

John was certain Platt was lying. He claimed he'd been at a bar, but there was no odor of alcohol about him, and in the cold, still air he would have detected it on his breath.

"The closest bar is over a mile away," said John, "and you're telling me you hiked there in your shirtsleeves in the dead of winter, right?"

"Yup. I like the cold. It don't bother me a bit."

John took him by the arm. "Come with me," he said. "We're going to take a little walk."

Veto and Dominick were asleep inside their Dodge Ram when John tapped on the windshield with his aluminum flashlight.

Veto jerked erect and rolled his window down. He wiped a hand over his face and blinked groggily at John. "Must have fallen asleep," he said. "What time is it, anyway?"

"Twelve o'clock," said John.

Dominick leaned forward and peeked around Veto. "Who's that you got with you?" he said, rubbing the sleep from his eyes.

"His name is Jason Platt. Recognize him?"

"That's not the guy we saw in the headlights," said Veto. "But he might be the other one." He turned his head toward his partner. "What do you think, Dominick?"

"Might be," he parroted. "He's the same size as the guy who ran into the woods. Same beard too."

John suspected their response. Still, he couldn't help feeling a twinge of disappointment when they couldn't place him with the deer.

"Jason and I are going to take a short trip up the road," he told them. "After that I'll be heading down to his camp. Would you be willing to come along? See if you can ID anyone?"

"Absolutely," said Veto. "We're here for the long haul."

"Thanks. I'll be back soon."

John escorted Jason Platt to his patrol car and had him sit in the passenger seat. After securing Platt's seatbelt, he walked to the driver's side, opened the door and slid inside. Pennsylvania game wardens don't have partition cages in their vehicles, which makes the task of transporting prisoners potentially dangerous. Although Platt remained in handcuffs, John kept him well within in his peripheral vison as he drove up the narrow mountain road.

"Where you taking me?" asked Platt.

"The bar."

"Why, you need a drink?" he snorted.

John ignored the comment and focused on the road ahead.

After a moment Platt said, "Okay, bad joke. So why the bar?"

"That's where you were before I stopped you, right?"

"Yeah. So?"

"I want to see if anyone remembers you."

They were on the road less than ten minutes when John turned on his left blinker and pulled into the Trailz End Bar and Grill, a cottage-style wood-planked building that was surrounded by state forest and looked more like a hunting cabin than anything else. The only bar, or eatery for that matter, to be found within ten miles. It was a weekday, and only a few vehicles were there. John pulled up to the front door and parked, then he reached over and unlatched Platt's seatbelt.

Platt's face was incredulous. "You're not taking me inside, are you?"

"Yep."

"In handcuffs?"

"Yep."

John got out of his patrol car, walked around to the passenger side, and opened Platt's door. "Let's go," he said.

Platt slid off his seat and stood next to John with his hands cuffed behind his back. "Why are you treating me like this? I ain't no criminal, man."

John took him by the arm. "Poaching is a crime," he said. "So I guess that remains to be seen."

The smell of stale beer was thick in the air, the floor sticky with layers of spilled alcohol as they stepped inside the dark and dingy bar. The place was empty save three men who sat at a wooden table by the door playing poker and smoking cigarettes while nursing bottles of beer. They gawked with open surprise as a uniformed game warden walked past them with his prisoner. The bartender stood at the far end of the bar and stared curiously as they approached. She was a beefy woman in her fifties with shoulder-length gray hair and a no-nonsense look about her.

"Can I help you?" she said in a gravelly voice.

John said, "Ever see this man before?"

She glanced at Platt and then back at the warden. "Nope."

Platt sat in gloomy silence as they drove toward his hunting camp. Veto and Dominick trailed behind in their Dodge Ram. John was now totally convinced that Jason Platt was one of the poachers responsible for killing the illegal doe. Still, without additional hard evidence to tie him into the crime, it would be almost impossible to get a conviction in court. And judging by Platt's sullen attitude, there was no way he was going to confess.

John had instructed Veto and Dominick to remain in their vehicle when they got to the camp. The plan was for John to go into the cabin and bring Platt's partner outside so they could get a look at him. He didn't want them tagging along when he approached the man. You could never tell how a poacher might react when confronted by a game warden in the wee hours of night, especially if he'd been drinking heavily.

When they arrived at Platt's cabin, the lights were on inside. As they pulled into the driveway and parked, a large picture window faced them, and they could see a man in a red shirt walk past it as he went for the door. He opened it and peeked outside, closing it immediately when he saw the warden's car.

John shut off his engine and turned to Platt. "What's your friend's name?"

Platt stared at John, his face expressing uncertainty as to whether he should answer.

"A little cooperation on your part might help you later on," said John. "I'm only asking for a name."

Platt thought for a moment, then shrugged. "It's Chet Patterson. But he didn't do nothing, just like me."

John left Jason Platt shackled inside his vehicle and walked over to Veto's truck. "Did you see the guy at the cabin door?"

"Yep," said Veto. "Same person we saw in the headlights."

"I'm going to try talking to him. If he doesn't cooperate, would you be willing to come to court and testify?"

"Definitely," said Veto.

"You can count on me, too," agreed Dominick.

"Thanks," said John. "You should go and get some sleep. It'll be daylight in a few hours and you don't want to be snoozing when that trophy buck comes along."

Veto smiled. "Appreciate it, man. But we're staying here in case you need help."

"Okay," said John. "Just stay in your truck and keep your eye on Platt. If he starts kicking out my windows or does anything stupid, blast your horn and I'll come right out."

"You got it, man."

John walked over to the wood-framed cabin and knocked on the door. When there was no answer, he knocked harder, rattling the door on its hinges this time. "State Game Commission!" he called. "Come on out!"

He could hear footsteps approach and stepped to the side when he heard the metallic clack of a deadlatch sliding back.

Then the door swung open and Patterson's large frame filled the entranceway.

"State game warden," said John. "I want to talk to you about the deer you killed tonight."

"Deer I killed? I don't know anything about a deer!"

"That's not what Jason tells me," said John, hoping to make him think Platt had ratted him out.

Patterson's head jerked back in surprise, his eyes shifting to the warden's darkened patrol car.

"So you got Jason, huh?"

"That's right."

Patterson stared at the warden, nodding methodically. Then he shrugged and stepped back. "Might as well come inside," he said. "Too cold to be jawing out here anyway."

John stepped into the cabin and Chet Patterson closed the door behind them. "Look, warden," he said, "I don't care what Platt told you; I wasn't involved with any deer. If he got himself in trouble and wants to confess, that's fine by me. But I was here all night."

Although John had spotted the cased hunting knife hanging from Patterson's belt when he first opened the door, he made no move to take it and had been careful to keep his distance. Now, in the full interior light of the cabin, he could see small traces of dried blood on the leather sheath.

"Why would Jason say you were involved with the deer if you weren't?" asked John. "Aren't you two friends?"

Patterson shrugged. "Jason and me haven't been getting along lately. He thinks I'm seeing his girl behind his back. He brought it up earlier tonight. I denied it of course, but he didn't believe me and stormed out the door in a rage. I ain't seen him since. Matter of fact, we got three other guys staying here, and they're out looking for him right now."

John wondered if the three other guys were the poker players he saw eyeballing him in the bar.

"So that's your story, huh?" said John.

"That's right. Platt's just trying to get me in trouble because he thinks I'm seeing his girl. Look, it's my word against his, okay? And I'm telling you, I wasn't involved with any deer tonight!"

John said, "Did you see the Dodge Ram parked outside?"

"Yeah, I saw it."

"Look familiar?"

"Nope."

"There are two men inside that truck who say you're the person they saw with a deer in the cemetery tonight."

"I don't care what they say. I was here all night. So don't waste my time with any more questions, because I got nothing else to say."

John nodded soberly. "Understood. Now, slowly and carefully, unbuckle your belt and let that knife fall to the floor."

Patterson's brow narrowed with unease. "What?"

"Just do it," commanded John.

The warden's tone was acid. And although his hand hadn't made the slightest movement toward it, Patterson couldn't help but notice the heavy Smith and Wesson revolver hanging from his hip. Patterson reached down and unbuckled his belt, allowing it to fall to the floor along with his sheathed knife.

"Now kick it over to me."

Patterson complied. The belt slid across the smooth wooden floor, stopping inches from John's feet. He stooped to pick it up, his eyes on Patterson all the while. With two fingers, he pulled the bone-handled knife partially from its sheath. The blade was encrusted with dried blood. Two thin deer hairs were stuck to the gore. John slid the knife back into the sheath and slipped it free from Patterson's belt, then he stuffed it into a back pocket.

"Where's your hunting license?" he said.

"On the table behind you. Jason's too. They're under the hunting magazine."

John took two steps back to a small coffee table and saw a dated copy of *Sports Afield*. He moved it aside. Finding two hunting licenses underneath, he took them both.

Patterson looked stunned. "You're confiscating our licenses?"

"Relax," said John. "I'll give them back after I'm finished taking the information I need."

"Need for what?"

"Your citations for the illegal deer."

"No way, pal!" growled Patterson. "I'll see you in court! And then I'm gonna sue you for harassment. You got no business hassling me like this!"

John walked to the cabin door and opened it. Then he turned and tossed Patterson's belt to him. "Better put it on," he said. "Your pants are falling down."

John expected his case would end up in court, and prepared his evidence for the forensics lab by packaging Patterson's knife along with a tissue sample from the illegal deer into two separate plastic bags. He placed both bags into a heavy manila envelope and stapled a yellow evidence tag to it. The yellow tag was an integral component of the chain of possession that every law enforcement officer must follow when handing evidence over to another agency. Each tag is individually numbered and contains a range of information about the case, including the suspect's name, date and time of the alleged violation, and a description of the contents. After placing the envelope into a refrigerated shipping box, he enclosed an Evidence Submittal Form listing his instructions as follows:

Item Description:

Item #1: Plastic envelope containing knife taken from suspect with blood, tissue and hair.

Item #2: Plastic envelope containing blood, tissue and hair taken from whitetail deer found in cemetery

Special Examination Instructions:

Determine if blood, tissue and hair in item #1 are from a whitetail deer.

Determine if DNA from Item #1 matches DNA in item #2.

If everything turned out the way John expected, when the results came back, he'd be able to show the court that the blood and hair on Chet Patterson's knife matched the blood and hair taken from the illegal doe discovered in the cemetery.

John forwarded the evidence via UPS Air, next day service, to the United States Fish & Wildlife Forensics Laboratory in Ashland, Oregon. After waiting the better part of a year for the results, he finally received a reply in the mail. It arrived via Federal Express in a large blue envelope marked United States Department of the Interior—Fish and Wildlife Service. Opening the envelope, he found a two-page document inside titled GENETICS EXAMINATION REPORT. His eyes pored over it, searching for the final results, but the first page simply detailed how the examination had been conducted at the lab. John flipped to the second page, dropping his eyes to the final paragraph. It said **CONCLUSION:** *LAB-1 and LAB-2 originated from the same individual North American Whitetail Deer.*

Now certain that he had enough evidence to convict Chet Patterson, he filed criminal charges against him for the possession of an unlawfully killed deer (because there was no physical evidence tying Jason Platt to the case, he was never charged). In return, Patterson requested a hearing in front of the local district justice, thinking there was no way he could be convicted of killing the deer if nobody saw him shoot it. But what Patterson didn't realize is that John didn't have to prove he actually killed the deer. Possession of the unlawfully killed deer, in itself, was punishable by a five-hundred dollar fine plus the loss of his hunting and trapping privileges for three years.

Once the trial date was set, John struggled with the idea of just how to present the DNA evidence in court. If he tried to submit the lab report without testimony from the accompanying forensic scientist, Patterson's attorney would likely object. If the judge went along with the objection, which John believed he would, his case would be dismissed. But flying a forensic specialist from Oregon to Pennsylvania to testify in court would be expensive. He wondered if his agency would foot the bill. But to his surprise, when he called the US Fish and Wildlife Service to determine the costs, they were more than willing to pay for the flight plus all other federal expenses involved with the hearing. As it turned out, because DNA evidence was so new, their chief forensic scientist needed to testify in as many states as possible in order to establish enough credible background to qualify as an expert witness in DNA trials throughout the country, and they were eager to add Pennsylvania to their catalog of states.

Three months after filing charges against Chet Patterson, John found himself sitting in front of a judge along with Veto and Dominick and a forensic scientist that had flown over two thousand miles across the country to testify for the Game Commission. Patterson was there too, shackled and wearing an orange jumpsuit after being escorted into the courtroom by two sheriff's deputies. He'd been in jail for some unrelated crime, and it seemed he just couldn't keep out of trouble with the law. Still, he was entitled to an attorney, and a court-appointed defense lawyer had been assigned to him.

"Is the Commonwealth ready?" asked the judge.

"Yes, Your Honor," John replied.

John was first to take the stand. He testified at length about the information he'd received from Veto and Dominick regarding the two men they'd seen with a deer, and how they'd fled when spotted, one of them wearing a red shirt as he ran in front of Veto's headlights. John said that Chet Patterson was that person, pointing to Patterson as he told the judge how he'd been identified by Veto and Dominick when they saw him standing in the open doorway of his cabin that night. He went on to testify about the bloody knife he confiscated from Patterson's belt, and the procedure he'd used to submit it to the United States Fish & Wildlife Service along with blood samples taken from the illegal deer.

In return, Patterson's attorney asked a number of questions in a spirited attempt to trip John up, but he finally abandoned the notion and John stepped down from the witness stand to call Jim LeMay as his next witness.

After being duly sworn, LeMay took the stand and answered some questions John put forward in order to have him accepted as an expert witness by the court. He testified at length about his degree in medical technology and his years of experience with the Fish and Wildlife Service along with his coauthored publications and professional presentations regarding DNA and forensics. When he finished, Patterson's attorney agreed that he would stipulate to LeMay's expertise, and the judge concurred, granting that LeMay would be considered an expert in DNA and forensic science in his courtroom.

Taking two copies of LeMay's lab report regarding his DNA analysis from a folder, John handed one to the judge and another to Patterson's attorney. Then he took two manila evidence envelopes from his desktop, walked to the witness stand, and handed them to LeMay.

"Mr. LeMay," he said, "I want to show you what has been marked as Commonwealth Exhibit Numbers One and Two, and ask you to identify them for the Court."

LeMay: "These are the two envelopes containing items that I analyzed for the Pennsylvania Game Commission. The envelope marked *Item One* had a hunting knife containing blood, tissue and hair taken from a suspect. The envelope marked *Item Two* contained another sample of blood, tissue and hair taken from a deer in a cemetery."

John: "And could you tell the court what the results were?"

LeMay: "Yes. The species determination identified the two items as originating from the same individual North American whitetail deer."

John: "So, you're testifying today that the blood and hair on the defendant's knife came from the deer in the cemetery."

LeMay: "Yes."

John: "To what degree of certainty are you able to say this?"

LeMay: "I can't give you a degree of certainty, but I can give you a probability of identity. And that probability of identity is that there is a one-in-ten-thousand chance that there might be another deer in this state that exhibits that same profile."

John: "The entire state, you say, not just Clinton County. Correct?"

LeMay: "Yes."

John: "Thank you, Mr. LeMay. No further questions, Your Honor."

The judge looked at Patterson's attorney. "Any cross examination, counselor?"

The defense attorney knew that LeMay's testimony concerning the blood evidence was overwhelming. In just a few short sentences, he'd proven that Patterson's knife had been used to gut the illegal doe. And that, coupled with the fact that Veto and Dominick could place Patterson at the scene, all but ensured a guilty verdict. "I'd like to confer with my client for a moment," he said.

"Proceed, but make it short," the judge said sternly.

Patterson whipped his head toward the attorney, his face frozen in a scowl of defiance as he grumbled something under his breath. The attorney replied, speaking in low tones, shaking his head emphatically. Patterson looked over at John and LeMay, then back at his lawyer. Additional words were exchanged, more heated this time, the attorney stabbing his finger at the lab report on his desk. Patterson stared at him for a long moment, then he nodded in submission and bowed his head. The conversation had taken less than a minute when the defense attorney stood from his desk and addressed the judge.

"No further questions, Your Honor."

The judge leaned back in his chair for a moment and nodded his head with slow and reflective deliberation. Then he looked directly at Chet Patterson.

"This trial has ended. Mr. Patterson," he said, "and there will be no leniency. I sentence you to the maximum penalty of a five-hundred dollar fine plus court costs and three years revocation of your hunting and trapping privileges. You can make arrangements to pay your fine and costs with my secretary before you leave today. If you can't pay the fine and costs, you can remain in jail for an additional ninety days beyond whatever is left of your present sentence."

With that, the judge arose from his desk and walked out of the courtroom into his private chambers. John and his witnesses stepped out as well, leaving Patterson alone with his attorney and the sheriff's deputies who would escort him back to the county jail.

And so it was that my identical twin brother became the first game warden in the history of Pennsylvania to successfully prosecute a poaching case using DNA evidence. I was proud of him then and I'm proud of him to this day. For we are Blood, he and I.

Published June 1998

William Wasserman, a third-degree black belt in Korean karate and a former national bodybuilding champion, has written eight books about his life as a state game warden. He received numerous awards for his work in wildlife conservation, including the United Bowhunters of Pennsylvania Game Protector of the Year Award, Pennsylvania Game Commission Northeast Region Outstanding Wildlife Conservation Officer, National Society Daughters of the American Revolution Conservation Medal, and the Pennsylvania Trappers Association Presidential Award. Wasserman has been published in several national magazines including *Black Belt, Pennsylvania Game News, Fur-Fish-Game, South Carolina Wildlife, International Game Warden,* and *The Alberta Game Warden.* Wasserman retired from the Pennsylvania Game Commission after thirty-two years of dedicated service and lives in South Carolina with his wife, Maryann.

BY WILLIAM WASSERMAN

TRACK OF THE
POACHER

WILLIAM WASSERMAN

BY WILLIAM WASSERMAN

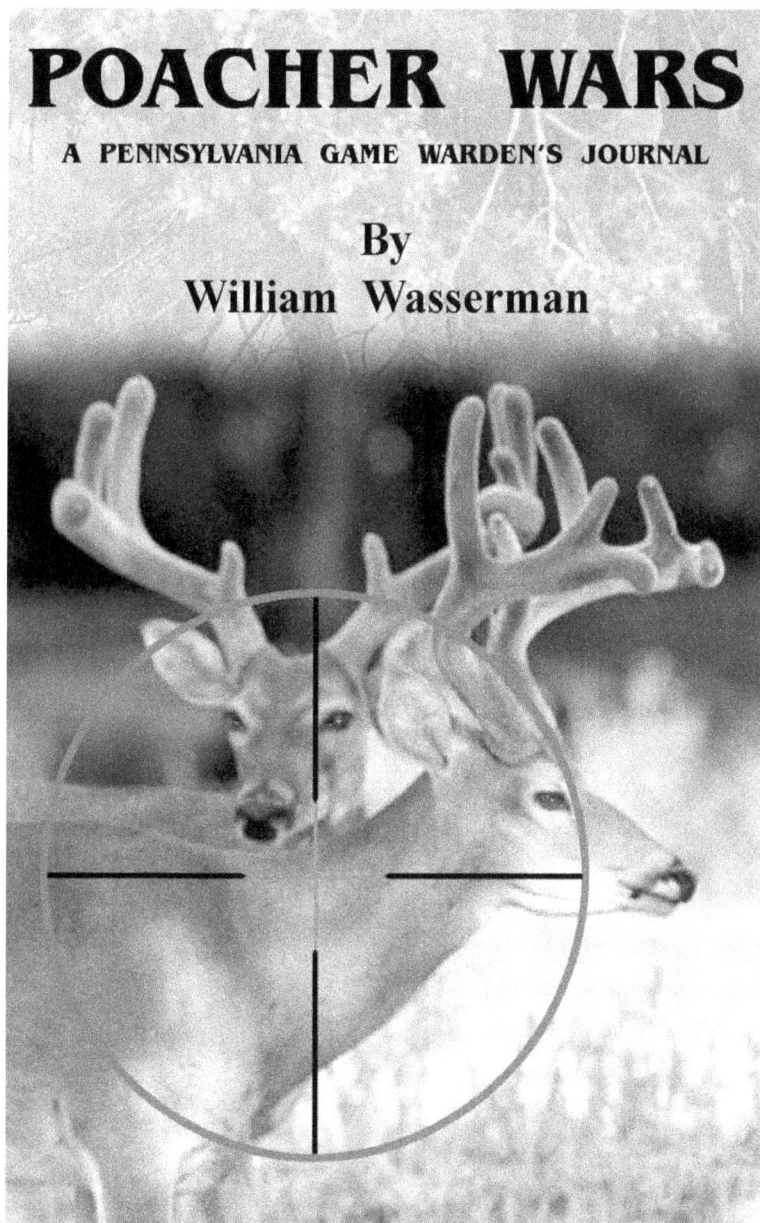

POACHER WARS

A PENNSYLVANIA GAME WARDEN'S JOURNAL

By
William Wasserman